Copyright 1998 by Time Inc. Home Entertainment
Published by TIME Books
Time Inc., 1271 Ave. of the Americas, New York, NY 10020
Library of Congress Catalog Card Number: 98-85391
ISBN #1-883013-39-9

Printed in the United States of America

TIME

1923-1998

75 YEARS

AN ANNIVERSARY CELEBRATION

CONTENTS

20

34

56

74

75 Years

Editor	Kelly Knauer
Art Director	Anthony Wing Kosner
Picture Editor	Patricia Cadley
Research Director	Leah Shanks Gordon
Essays	Alan Brinkley, Howard Chua-Eoan, George J. Church, Robert Hughes, Richard Lacayo, Lance Morrow, Walter Isaacson, Michael Kinsley, Bruce W. Nelan, Eric Pooley
Copy Editor	Bruce Christopher Carr
Production Director	John Calvano
Photo Technology	Urbano DelValle
Research Assistant	Rudi Papiri
TIME Special Projects Editor	Barrett Seaman

Special thanks to: TIME Director of Photography Michele Stephenson, Art Director Arthur Hochstein and Cover Coordinator Linda Louise Freeman for their assistance with the sections on photojournalism and cover art in TIME

And thanks to: Ames Adamson, Ken Baierlein, Andy Blau, Dick Duncan, Elena Falaro, Paula Gillen, Bill Hooper, Ed Jamieson, Kevin Kelly, Amy Musher, Adrianne J. Navon, Robert Stephens, Cornelis Verwaal, Miriam Winocur, Anna Yelenskaya

TIME INC. HOME ENTERTAINMENT

President	David Gitow
Director, Continuities and Single Sales	David Arfine
Director, Continuities and Retention	Michael Barrett
Director, New Products	Alicia Longobardo
Group Product Managers	Robert Fox, Michael Holahan
Product Managers	Christopher Berzolla, Roberta Harris, Stacy Hirschberg, Jennifer McLyman, Daniel Melore
Manager, Retail and New Markets	Thomas Mifsud
Associate Product Managers	Alison Ehrmann, Carlos Jiminez, Daria Rachse, Betty Su, Cheryl Zukowski
Assistant Product Managers	Meredith Shelley, Lauren Zaslansky
Editorial Operations Director	John Calvano
Fulfillment Director	Michelle Gudema
Assistant Fulfillment Manager	Richard Perez
Financial Director	Tricia Griffin
Associate Financial Manager	Amy Maselli
Assistant Financial Manager	Steven Sandonato

CONSUMER MARKETING DIVISION

Book Production Manager	Jessica McGrath
Book Production Coordinator	Joseph Napolitano

We welcome your comments and suggestions about TIME Books. Please write to us at:

TIME Books
Attention: Book Editors
P.O. Box 11016
Des Moines, IA 50336-1016

If you would like to order additional copies of any of our books, please call us at 1-800-327-6388
(Monday through Friday 7:00 a.m.–8:00 p.m. or Saturday 7:00 a.m.–6:00 p.m. Central Time)

WHILE THIS BOOK CONTAINS MANY NEW ARTICLES CREATED to celebrate TIME's 75th anniversary, most of its pages reprint stories and pictures from the magazine's archives. In the interest of authenticity, these stories have been printed just as they originally appeared, although in a few cases some words have been removed to fit a story. These minor changes are marked in the text. The original wording of the stories has not been altered, even though some terminologies of the past may offend readers today. Likewise, all original spellings have been retained—thus our Man of the Year 1978, Teng Hsiao-p'ing, is also our Man of the Year 1985, Deng Xiaoping.

A note on dates: the issue dates that follow the archival passages may give the incorrect impression that TIME's coverage lags 10 or 12 days behind events. Reason: the issues are dated one week ahead, to indicate the last day they will appear on newsstands. So, for instance, TIME's coverage of the bombing of the Murrah Federal Building in Oklahoma City on April 19, 1995, appeared in the issue that was published April 24 and dated May 1.

Kelly Knauer

FROM TIME'S EARLIEST YEARS, THE LETTERS COLUMN that leads the magazine each week has been popular with readers–so popular that for several years in the 1930s, Time Inc. published a fortnightly supplement to TIME consisting entirely of letters from readers. Today TIME receives about 1,400 letters each week, some 25% of which are sent via e-mail. One reason for the enduring appeal of the Letters section: many of the newsmakers featured in the magazine's pages write in to take issue with TIME's reporting. A number of the most memorable of these retorts follow.

SEPT. 28, 1925

IS THE GLORIFICATION OF THE NEGRO NOW an accepted policy of your magazine? I had hoped that after the protest of one Southerner you might show some consideration for the sensibilities of our people by the discontinuance of your practice of referring to the colored man as "mister." I was deeply grieved, therefore, to find two new instances of this kind in your Sept. 7 issue. This practice, in the face of previous protest, impresses me as a flagrant affront to the feelings of our people. If it be your desire to alienate and force from your ranks such readers of TIME as hail from the South, you are pursuing a most effectual course.

Barlow Henderson
Aiken, S.C.

It is not TIME's desire to lose the good will of its Southern friends. TIME will, however, continue to employ the "Mr." in referring to men who lack other titles. Would Mr. Henderson himself care to be styled plain "Henderson"? —ED.

JAN. 11, 1932

I WAS IN THE CLASS OF '86 AT HARVARD. I was not expelled in '87 nor any other year. I never did anything very bad at Harvard nor anything very good either. I was rusticated in '86 for an excess of political enthusiasm and a certain deficiency in intellectual attainments. I did not return to be graduated. There did not seem to be either reason or hope. I think the less said about my college career the better. Perhaps that is so with the rest of my career. However, exercise your own judgment, only please print the facts, or perhaps I should say, please don't.

William Randolph Hearst
Los Angeles, Calif.

Rustication: An old-fashioned academic penalty whereby delinquent or intractable undergraduates are sent away, generally to their homes to continue their studies under a supervisor designated by the college. —ED.

W.R. Hearst
Jan. 11, 1932

Harpo Marx
Sept. 14, 1936

AUG. 6, 1934

I DO NOT KNOW WHEN I EVER SAW SUCH A conglomeration of lies. The 638 was not the engine my husband was killed on and was never a passenger engine, and as to my son being a highway laborer, that was a base lie; he was never on a highway in his life unless he drove over it. Whoever gave you the information did not get it from me. I just want to tell you that I do not like one thing you said and please never attempt it again without my permission.

Mrs. Casey Jones
Jackson, Tenn.

SEPT. 14, 1936

I CAN TALK BUT I HATE TO INTERRUPT Groucho. I spoke in public last year in Portland when I asked for a raise in salary but I don't think anyone heard me. I make a practice of speaking every time Chico makes a grand slam, so you can look for another speech in 1937. Regret I can't get Zeppo in this wire.

Harpo Marx
Culver City, Calif.

OCT. 11, 1937

THE RECORDS ON "SPITTIN' IMAGE" SHOULD certainly be kept straight. I don't think that the expression has anything to do with saliva. It originated, I believe, among the darkies of the South and the correct phrasing—without dialect—is "spirit and image." It was originally used in speaking of some person whose father had passed on—and the colored folks would say—"the very spi't an' image of his daddy."

Joel Chandler Harris Jr.
Atlanta, Ga.

JAN. 5, 1942

TIME USED THE WORDS "YELLOW BAStards" [*see page 66 in this book*] and "Hitler's little yellow friends" in speaking of the Japanese. I suggest that none of us use the word "yellow" in speaking of the Japanese, because our Allies, the Chinese, are yellow.

In this war we must, I think, take care not to divide ourselves into color groups. The tide of feeling about color runs very high over in the Orient. Indians, Chinese,

Filipinos, and others are sensitive to the danger point about their relation as colored peoples to white peoples. Many Americans do not realize this, but it is true, and we must recognize it or we may suffer for it severely. The Japanese are using our well-known race prejudice as one of their chief propaganda arguments against us. Everything must be done to educate Americans not to provide further fuel for such Japanese propaganda.

Pearl S. Buck
Perkasie, Pa.

TIME emphatically agrees with Novelist Pearl Buck that raising a race issue is as unwise as it is ignoble. However, "yellow bastards" was not TIME's phrase but the factual report of typical angry reactions documented by correspondents all over the U.S. As for actual skin-color, U.S. white, pink or pale faces may well be proud to be fighting on the side of Chinese, Filipinos and other yellow or brown faces. —ED.

Pearl S. Buck
Jan. 5, 1942

Salvador Dalí
Jan. 18, 1943

JAN. 18, 1943

I APPRECIATE GREATLY THAT NOT ONCE was the word obscene mentioned in your article. Epithet too easily used which assailed unanimously the appearance of "Interpretation of Dreams" by Freud, psychologic document which is and always will remain in spite of all the most important and sensational of our epoch.

Salvador Dalí
Carmel, Calif.

MARCH 6, 1944

TIME'S STORY ON THE HOLLYWOOD Free World Association *v.* the Motion Picture Alliance for the Preservation of American Ideals indicates no editorial preference for either organization but reveals in comic style an anti-Hollywood bias. We film-makers realize our com-

Orson Welles
March 6, 1944

William F. Buckley Jr.
Aug. 20, 1945

munity is a gorgeous subject for satire. We grant, or anyway most of us do, that we are the world's funniest people. You can write more jokes about us than you can about plumbers, undertakers or Fuller brush salesmen. Hollywood is guilty of deliberate withdrawal from the living world. It seeks to entertain, and we suspect that the success of the withdrawal is what makes Hollywood funny. But let TIME Magazine view with alarm or point with pride, but not laugh off Hollywood's growing recognition of the fact that every movie expresses, or at least reflects, political opinion. Moviegoers live all over the world, come from all classes, and add up to the biggest section of human beings ever addressed by any medium of communication. The politics of moviemakers therefore is just exactly what isn't funny about Hollywood. TIME mentions "room-temperature burgundy and chopped chicken liver" as though these luxuries invalidate political opinion. TIME, whose editors eat chopped chicken liver and whose publishers drink room-temperature burgundy, knows better.

Orson Welles
Hollywood, Calif.

Well-fed TIME feels that the public should be kept informed about Hollywood politics, from soup to nuts. —ED.

AUG. 20, 1945

RE LETTER FROM ARMY SERGEANT'S Name Withheld in TIME in which Sgt. Withheld intimates that the Catholic Church is responsible for the disunity between the Americans and the Russians:

Catholics have been brought up to fear and dislike Communism because of its avowed ungodliness. As Catholics we are indeed convinced that Christianity

and Communism are irreconcilable in the same way that as Americans we believe that totalitarianism and democracy are incompatible.

Nevertheless, insofar as such an action does not interfere with our own way of life, we heartily ratify the action of our Government in joining hands with a state, no matter what color its banner, if such a union will further our aim of beating Japan. Few Quixotes still proclaim that this war is being fought for ideals, and I believe there is no American—Protestant, Catholic, etc.—who is unwilling to welcome any type government into an alliance which will cooperate in preventing future wars.

William F. Buckley Jr.
Lieutenant, U.S.A.
Camp Gordon, Ga.

JAN. 7, 1946

WHEN I HAVE A HIGHBALL OR TWO I TELL the truth about things. The truth, as you continually show in your pages, is tough. It is not then so much my talk that is tough as the stuff it deals with. But I'm not the town drunk. With the reputation you give me I'll be expected to drink everybody in Kansas City under the table and I can't do it—not me.

Thomas H. Benton
Kansas City

Said TIME: "Tom Benton, who does know how to drink..." No town drunk does. —ED.

Thomas H. Benton
Jan. 17, 1946

Humphrey Bogart
Nov. 8, 1948

NOV. 8, 1948

IT HAS COME TO MY ATTENTION THAT IN your Current & Choice section, Lauren Bacall has consistently been left out of the cast of *Key Largo*. Inasmuch as there are those of us in Hollywood, Miss Bacall among them, who would rather make Current & Choice than win an Academy Award or make Men of Distinction, won't you please include her in the cast of *Key Largo* in Current & Choice just once, as she is my wife and I have to live with her. Miss Bacall is extremely tired of being labeled *et al.*

Humphrey Bogart
Beverly Hills, Calif.

JAN. 17, 1949

I DIDN'T KNOW I HAD BEEN HIRED and fired by *Theatre Arts* until I read about it in TIME. What else has been happening to me lately that I ought to know about?

William Saroyan
New York City

TIME regrets that it is fresh out of Saroyan news. All that the present editor [Charles MacArthur] of *Theatre Arts* knows about this crisis in American letters is that it occurred while he was in Europe and that he remains as ever Mr. Saroyan's most faithful fan. —ED.

William Saroyan
Jan. 17, 1949

Aldous Huxley
Aug. 30, 1954

AUG. 30, 1954

YOU INFORM YOUR READERS THAT IN MY last book [*The Doors of Perception*], I "prescribe mescaline, a derivative of peyote, for all mankind as an alternative to cocktails." Snappiness, alas, is apt to be in inverse ratio to accuracy. In actual fact, I did not prescribe mescaline for all mankind. I merely suggested that it might be a good thing if psychologists, sociologists and pharmacologists were to get together and discuss the problem of a satisfactory drug for general consumption. Mescaline, I said, would not do. But a chemical possessing the merits of mescaline without its drawbacks

would certainly be preferable to alcohol.

Aldous Huxley
Hampstead, London

Fred Astaire
May 26, 1958

Miriam Makeba
Feb. 29, 1960

MAY 26, 1958

I'D LIKE TO GIVE MY OPINION OF THE Kokoschka picture of my sister. I think it's a hideous mess. As great an artist as this man may be today, he certainly goofed in 1926. My sister is a very pretty girl.

Fred Astaire
Beverly Hills

FEB. 29, 1960

THERE WAS A SLIGHT ERROR, WHICH I DO not think you will mind my calling attention to. It concerns my African name. I would like to spell it correctly for you:

Zenzile Makeba Qgwashu Nguvama Yiketheli Nxgowa Bantana Balomzi Xa Ufun Ubajabulisa Ubaphekeli, Mbiza Yotshwala Sithi Xa Saku Qgiba Ukutja Sithathe Izitsha Sizi Khabe Singama Lawu Singama Qgwashu Singama Nqamla Nqgithi.

The reason for its length is that every child takes the first name of all his male ancestors. Often following the first name is a descriptive word or two, telling about the character of the person, making a true African name somewhat like a story.

Miriam Makeba
New York City

FEB. 24, 1961

I AM GLAD TO SEE YOU ARE STILL BATTING 1.000 regarding any information concerning me. As usual your information stinks. I need a house and a nightclub in Palm Beach like you need a tumor.

Frank Sinatra
Beverly Hills, Calif.

TIME reported: "Word appeared in the columns that Sinatra was about to buy a Palm Beach pad and a nightclub, too, so he could wage war with an established nightclub owner who had refused to offer Frankie $5,000 for a one-shot appearance."

APRIL 6, 1962

POEM TO THE BOOK REVIEW AT TIME:
You will keep hiring
        picadors
        from the back row
and pic the bull back
        far along his spine
        you will slam sandbags
        to the kidneys
        and pass a wine
poisoned on the vine

you will saw the horns off
        and murmur
        the bulls are
        ah
        the bulls are not
        what once they were
The corrida will end
        with Russians in the plaza
Swine, some of you will say
        what did we wrong?
And go forth to kiss
        the conquerors

Norman Mailer
New York City

Frank Sinatra
Feb. 24, 1961

Norman Mailer
April 6, 1962

MAY 21, 1965

AS AN ANTI-AMERICAN, I THANK YOU FOR your rotten article devoted to my person. Your insult to a head of state and your odious lies dishonor not only your magazine but also your nation …

I assure you that I would much prefer to die from the blows of the Communists (who are certainly hostile to royalty, but who have no contempt for us) than capitulate before you, who symbolize the

Norodom Sihanouk
May 21, 1965

Ronald Reagan
July 21, 1967

worst in humanity, *i.e.*, racism, discrimination, injustice, death and lies.

Norodom Sihanouk
Chief of State
Pnompenh, Cambodia

APRIL 1, 1966

ON THE CURRENT COVER OF TIME MAGazine my name appears, along with the titles of many of the shows I have produced. There is, however, a very strange drawing of some person or other also on the cover, which is very puzzling to me. Could you possibly have substituted, in error, next week's cover picture in place of mine? I consider this figure you have attached to my name monstrous in appearance, bearing no resemblance to my likeness, which appears on the inside in the body of my story—the one in which I am attired in my Ascot suit, the one I wore when I played the lead in *My Fair Lady*. Therefore, this is to notify you that I am suing you for $1,000,000 for defamation of caricature.

David Merrick
New York City

JULY 21, 1967

TIME OWES IT TO ITS READERS TO NAME the anonymous Governor whom I allegedly told that "Dick Nixon is a loser." It will be especially interesting, since I have never said it or thought it. I am sorry that at a time when Republican leaders are working hard for party unity, TIME would stoop to quoting nameless sources in an effort to destroy that unity.

Ronald Reagan
Governor
Sacramento, Calif.

TIME's source is not at all "nameless," but we are bound to honor his request that he not be identified—a request with which Governor Reagan, as a political figure, can surely sympathize.

SEPT. 5, 1969

RE YOUR COMMENT ... GEORGE SANDERS didn't divorce me, I divorced him.

Zsa Zsa Gabor
Washington, D.C.

True enough. Sanders filed to divorce Zsa Zsa and she then cross-complained, whereupon the judge ruled "ladies first" and granted her an interlocutory decree on April 1, 1954.

JAN. 4, 1971

THE CHILDREN AND I HAVE ALWAYS understood the significance of my husband's work and would have preferred to ignore Mr. Hoover's ungentlemanly attacks on my husband, but my husband is dead and cannot reply for himself. Moreover, his memory is too precious to us and to tens of millions of Americans, black and white, to permit unfounded slurs to remain unanswered. J. Edgar Hoover, in alleging that he called my husband a liar during their meeting in 1964, has exposed himself. There were witnesses present, three distinguished clergymen, who explicitly denied that Mr. Hoover made such a statement or any other attack on my husband's veracity to his face.

It is unfortunate for our country that a person of such moral and mental capacity holds a position of such importance. It is equally unfortunate for race relations that a person revealed in this interview to be so arrogantly prejudiced against Puerto Ricans, Mexicans and blacks is a high Government official.

Mrs. Martin Luther King Jr.
Atlanta

Zsa Zsa Gabor
Sept. 5, 1969

Mrs. M.L. King Jr.
Jan. 4, 1971

JAN. 1, 1973

WHOSE VOICE GAVE TARZAN'S CALL? I ought to know: I was there. Johnny Weissmuller can—and did—do his own Tarzan call. End of discussion?

Maureen O'Sullivan ("Jane")
New York City

APRIL 8, 1974

Maureen O'Sullivan
Jan. 1, 1973

Clare Boothe Luce
April 8, 1974

HARRY REASONER RECENTLY TOOK TIME TO task on ABC-TV for certain instances of its obsessional and below-the-belt reporting on Watergate, which he said had betrayed the canons of both objective and ethical journalism.

It was predictable that sooner or later TIME would begin to pay the price for its editorial overinvestment in the destruction of the President. That price, as Reasoner noted, is the loss of journalistic prestige and credibility. How ironic, and how fitting, that a distinguished media colleague and certified Nixon critic like Reasoner should blow the whistle on TIME for its phobic Watergate reporting!

No President of the U.S. except Lincoln (in retrospect, now to be considered another impeachable character) has ever been more savaged by the press than Nixon. For one solid year the press has been beating on him mercilessly. And he has shown that he can take it and take it and take it, with cool and courage. But few journalists—none on TIME—have had even the sportsmanship, no less the journalistic objectivity, to report that whatever Nixon is or is not, he is one helluva gutsy fighter.

Clare Boothe Luce
Honolulu

DEC. 15, 1975

ALTHOUGH I APPRECIATE YOUR UNEQUIV-ocal "No" answer to the question of my alleged presence in Dallas at the time of J.F.K.'s murder, I would like to point out that my noninvolvement rests not only on "drastic differences" between the specimen photographs, but more conclusively upon the sworn testimony of several witnesses who confirm that I was in Washington, D.C., on Nov. 22, 1963. It is a physical law that an object can occupy only one space at one time.

Correction: I am not a Watergate "burglar," but a conspirator.

Howard Hunt, Fed. Prison Camp
Eglin A.F.B., Fla.

Howard Hunt
Dec. 15, 1975

Jesse Jackson
May 3, 1976

MAY 3, 1976

YOU QUOTED ME AND IDENTIFIED ME AS A "black leader." I consider this journalistic racism. No one refers to George Wallace as a "white Governor" or Gerald Ford as a "white President." If a label must be attached to my leadership, as a minister of the gospel I prefer "moral leader." Moral leadership, which essentially deals with ideas and values, is a universal category. Black is not.

(The Rev.) Jesse L. Jackson
Chicago

AUG. 11, 1980

JUST TO KEEP THE RECORD STRAIGHT: I do not buy $5,000 dresses; I do not have an extensive jewelry collection, or paintings, or antiques; and I do not have a hairdresser and interior decorator in tow. I get my hair done once a week, and I'm at a loss as to what an interior decorator would do. Perhaps rearrange the furniture in all

Nancy Reagan
Aug. 11, 1980

Ansel Adams
July 27, 1981

the Holiday Inns I've been staying in.
Nancy Reagan
Pacific Palisades, Calif.

JULY 27, 1981

YOUR ESSAY "LOOKING STRAIGHT AT THE Bomb" reveals the dilemma we face because of "no thought" and the inability of our leaders to dare to spend billions for peace negotiations rather than for armaments and bravado. Mr. Reagan and his circle should remember that pride goeth before a fall.

Ansel Adams
Carmel, Calif.

NOV. 2, 1981

J.D. REED'S REVIEW OF MY NOVEL *REIN-hart's Women*, being utterly favorable, is of course a model of good taste. But when, in the subsequent biographical notes, I am quoted as having said, "I am so into cooking that ... ," I must protest. I do not speak or write (except as parody) in the dreadful jargon in which "into" is lazily substituted for "interested in" or "involved in" or "dedicated to" or "fascinated by," any more than I should say "relationship" to mean a connection between a man and a woman, or "life-style" with reference to a way of life. Please permit me to correct the record, lest I be despised by my students at Yale—all of whom, incidentally, write in a language of commendable purity.

Thomas Berger
Palisades, N.Y.

MARCH 29, 1982

WRITING IN TIMESTYLE (WHICH, IN self-improvement, I hasten to adopt), R.Z. Sheppard judges my work to be, among

other shames, "made by high intelligence." That is the kiss of death.

Cynthia Ozick
New Rochelle, N.Y.

APRIL 2, 1984

I THINK YOUR ARTICLE "JOURNALESE AS A Second Tongue" is very good stuff. Obviously, however, space limitations prevented you from referring to that sort of political mission known as "fact finding." I went on such a mission once, found a fact, picked it up with my tweezers, and now keep it in a cigar box in my garage in case there is ever any demand for it.

The phrase "between a rock and a hard place" is, to my knowledge, a ruralism. I first heard it in Arizona about 1940 and had the impression it had been in use long before that. Country sayings almost invariably have a much higher poetic component than their big-city equivalents. Some of these observations have become classics, like "nervous as a long-tailed cat in a roomful of rockin' chairs." One of my particular favorites is "as lonesome as a peanut in a boxcar."

Steve Allen
Van Nuys, Calif.

Cynthia Ozick
March 29, 1982

Steve Allen
April 2, 1984

JAN. 21, 1985

PETER UEBERROTH AS MAN OF THE Year? Outrageous. Most of the world cannot even spell his name, let alone know him. Is the planet so emaciated in human leadership—the Mother Teresas and Geraldine Ferraros—that we have to adulate the American dollar? Let's vote for Cap Weinberger. He will blow us up and make such further nominations unnecessary.

Melvin M. Belli Sr.
San Francisco

OCT. 21, 1985

YOUR ARTICLE ENDORSES UNCRITICALLY the ridiculous claim that our expressions of concern about pornography and explicit violence somehow arise from

Tipper Gore
Oct. 21, 1985

Ann Landers
Sept. 18, 1989

uneasiness over social activism like the Live Aid concert. Surely you know better than that. Millions of parents like me who grew up with and love rock music are concerned about the new phenomenon of popular songs aimed at younger children that glorify sadomasochism, explicit sex, suicide, incest and the occult. The Parents Music Resource Center is opposed to any Government action to address this problem, but feels that the music industry has a responsibility to address it voluntarily.

Tipper Gore
Carthage, Tenn.

NOV. 25, 1985

CERTAINLY I AGREE WITH YOU THAT WE must preserve a sense of proportion and not panic over the spread of AIDS. After all, American aid has caused far more deaths in Viet Nam, Cambodia, Guatemala, Chile, El Salvador and Nicaragua, and no remedy has yet been found for this disease, in spite of efforts in Congress.

Graham Greene
Antibes, France

JAN. 20, 1986

WHEN AUTHOR CARLOS FUENTES, 57, WAS asked how he was enjoying his year at Harvard, he replied, "You don't have too much time to stop and say, 'Hey, I'm a celebrity,' because such things mean nothing in the face of death." I read the piece, shuddered, then ran my eyes back

over it, hoping to find a mention of cancer or some other dread affliction. No such luck. Fuentes was apparently referring to his age. I am 57 and feel happy and horny. Don't do this to me, Carlos.

Orson Bean
Venice, Calif.

SEPT. 18, 1989

MY NEGATIVE REMARKS ABOUT PSYCHIATRISTS were uncalled for. I know there are many dedicated, caring psychiatrists, and to have made such a sweeping generalization was absurd. I should have taken my own advice: Measure twice; saw once.

Ann Landers
Chicago

JAN. 3, 1994

YOUR ITEM "LARRY THE SHRINKING violet" noted that I had dropped by a party held by Treasury Secretary Lloyd Bentsen the night of the Administration's NAFTA victory. I was en route to a taping of my show at CNN, and I was not wearing a "cozy white warm-up outfit," as you said, but my usual on-air uniform: dress shirt, tie, suspenders, respectable dark dress trousers and my favorite baseball jacket, which celebrates Japan's Nippon Ham Fighters team. That didn't seem to bother anyone; President Clinton even asked where he could get a jacket like mine. I own no white warm-up outfits, cozy or otherwise. I always dress nice.

Larry King
Washington

Graham Greene
Nov. 25, 1985

Larry King
Jan. 3, 1994

OCT. 31, 1994

THE ARTICLE WRITTEN BY RICHARD Corliss, titled "The Last Leading Lady,

Jessica Tandy: 1909-1994," was not simply well written but was also so eloquent and so rewarding that I only wish I could have shared it with Jessie. In those last few weeks, when she wanted so desperately to die (never with tears, never with self-pity, but just because of exhaustion), I kept trying to remind her what an extraordinary success she had had as a wife, as a mother and as an actress. I hope that it registered and that in her darkest moments she may have remembered and even believed it.

Hume Cronyn
New York City

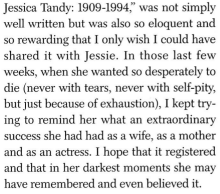

Hume Cronyn
Oct. 31, 1994

Geena Davis
Jan. 11, 1932

MARCH 25, 1996

FOR YEARS I WANTED TO MAKE THE cover of TIME in the worst way. And I did. On April 4, 1994, there I was, in mug-shot gray, looking worried over President Clinton's shoulder in the Oval Office, underneath an accusing headline: DEEP WATER: HOW THE PRESIDENT'S MEN TRIED TO HINDER THE WHITEWATER INVESTIGATION. The story wasn't much prettier than the picture. Two years later, nothing remains of the criminal charges leveled against me by anonymous sources in TIME except, of course, my yet-to-be paid legal bills …

George R. Stephanopoulos
Washington

JULY 14, 1997

I FELT BAD THAT YOU CALLED ME QUIRKY and deemed two of my movies "box-office poison." Then I noticed you said that Dennis Rodman's sometime religion is "Moron" and that Farrah Fawcett has Jell-O for brains. Now I realize it's an honor to be mentioned in such a classy magazine!

Geena Davis
Los Angeles

Lance Morrow

THE TIME OF OUR LIVES

MAGAZINE IS A LIVING THING. THE CHILD THAT BRITON Hadden and Henry Luce brought into the world in March 1923 was squally, bratty, brash. The new smart aleck—its voice distinctive, sophomoric, self-assured—thrived, almost from the start: born lucky. The magazine sailed through the 1920s as if the decade were a breezy shakedown cruise.

But the '20s ended traumatically, for almost everyone. In 1929 Hadden came down with a strep infection that reached his heart and killed him at age 31. Luce was left to carry on alone. The stock market crashed a few months later. And in the years that followed, there unfolded all the high, dark world history for which the magazine's epic rhetoric became a perfectly appropriate libretto: the Great Depression, World War II and the Holocaust, Hiroshima, the cold war and all the rest, down the decades.

TIME prospered all the more. The gravity of world news—especially the war—stimulated the magazine's reporting and its genius for packaging news. TIME became an influence in millions of American lives. It inspired a competitor, *Newsweek* (which began publication in 1933). It acquired siblings—FORTUNE (1930), LIFE (1936), *The March of Time* (1935), *Architectural Forum* (1932). Luce had a golden touch.

And so eventually, the Weekly Newsmagazine matured into an American institution, mentor to the questing middle class, keeper of a certain American self-image and expectation—America's superego, the child of Henry Luce, a presence infuriating to many but undeniably a force.

Eventually, Robert Hutchins, the president of the University of Chicago, went so far as to claim that TIME, with its siblings, did more to mold the American character than "the whole education system put together." Even Luce's old enemy William Randolph Hearst admitted, "There can no longer be any doubt that TIME is the world's outstanding journalistic venture to date."

TIME, like Luce, was alert to the nuances of American

1923 TIME's first issue, above, had Speaker of the House Joseph Cannon on the cover. In 1926, Hadden, left, and Luce, center, reviewed the first issue printed in Cleveland

1945 In World War II, G.I.s like this Marine in the Pacific read small "pony" editions of TIME

power, which, in a way, was the ultimate focus of the magazine's interest. Occasionally, TIME went against the grain of majority opinion, as when Luce, who came to dislike Franklin Roosevelt, pushed Wendell Willkie as the American hope in 1940, or when, after Luce's death in 1967, the magazine seemed to predict the wrong presidential "inevitabilities"—Maine's Edmund Muskie in 1972, say, or Texas' John Connally in '80. As a monitor connected to the nation's political generators, the magazine sometimes misinterpreted the vibrations. In general, however, its record for being right was pretty good.

TIME's greatest influence was exerted in forming the nation's attitudes, its political opinions and social conscience—especially in the decades after World War II. In the '60s, during Vietnam, TIME was caught in a general American dégringolade, a deconstruction of established authority from the President on down. In the '70s, TIME helped guide the nation through the trauma of Watergate and, as part of its role as moral counselor, published the only editorial in its history, urging Richard Nixon to resign.

Born of the Wasp male ascendancy in a self-confidently patriarchal age, the magazine (which routinely used the word men to mean everyone) has passed, along with its parent company, through a series of self-transformations, from an age of industry and structured authority into a post–cold war era of free-flowing information and diversity. After 3,900 weeks of telling the story of the most complicated century in history, the TIME that Hadden and Luce created turned 75 in March 1998, just two years before the turn of the millennium.

L UCE AND HADDEN, CLASSMATES OUT OF Hotchkiss and Yale, succeeded because they understood this truth: history may be complicated, as life is complicated, but the business of storytelling is simple. The young men said in their prospectus that their creation would be judged by "how much it gets off its pages into the minds of its readers." Sort the world into stories and carry them (facts, personalities, ideas, images, dramas, quirks, gossip, the details and energy of life) from Out There, where things happen, to In Here, inside the reader's consciousness, where stories turn into wonder, entertainment, cautionary experience, useful memory. The magazine's voice, Luce said, had three modes: "Everything in TIME should be either titillating or epic or supercurtly factual."

The titillating voice told of "cinemactresses," or "great and good friends" (TIME code for lovers) or other uber-brat coinages. As for the magazine's epic voice, it expressed, at its best, a disciplined,

1935 Debut of the newsreel *The March of Time.* The spin-off became a classic

moral understanding of history, an adult's steady gaze. In a brief introduction to the Victory section in the issue of Aug. 20, 1945, for example, TIME, in contemplating Hiroshima and Nagasaki, said this: "With the controlled splitting of the atom, humanity, already profoundly perplexed and disunified, was brought inescapably into a new age. The race had been won; the weapon had been used by those on whom civilization could best hope to depend; but the demonstration of power against living creatures created a bottomless wound in the living conscience of the race."

The "supercurtly factual" permeated the magazine. "There Are 00 Trees in Russia," ran the title of a famous 1964 piece in *Harper's* magazine on TIME's obsessive fact-gathering and -checking systems, implying that the magazine had a sinister itch to make reality conform, through the use of plug-in facts, to the editors' preconceptions. Fair enough on occasion, but a little captious overall, in light of the magazine's scrupulous and expensive attention to accuracy.

Luce possessed a kind of clairvoyance about history, a journalist's instinct but operating in a higher orbit than journalism usually achieves. Along with Hadden, he saw that America after the Great War was in a state of change that would create a natural audience for the kind of magazine they had in mind. The nation's cultural center of gravity was shifting. A newly emergent, restless urban middle class—often intellectually and socially insecure—was getting into business, making money, buying things.

In the new age of the automobile, the motion picture, the radio, Hadden and Luce detected a new consumers' appetite for motion, stimulation, variety. Traditional sources of information had become inadequate. Newspapers were local or regional and in any case offered only a patchwork of information. Magazines often were specialized, with a tendency toward fat and bloviation; they rarely offered news as news. None even set out to be comprehensive on a national and international scale.

TIME played brilliantly to the new American appetite. The magazine turned the news into saga, comedy, melodrama. The very compression of early TIMEstyle, invented almost entirely by Hadden, lent it an urgency of mannered telegraphese. John Martin, Hadden's cousin and an early writer and editor at the magazine, left this account of Hadden at work: "Brit would edit copy to eliminate unnecessary verbiage ... If you wrote something like 'in the nick of time,' five words, he might change it to 'in time's nick,' three words ... At all times he had by him a carefully annotated translation of the *Iliad*.

On the back cover, he had listed hundreds of words, especially verbs and the compound adjectives, which had seemed to him fresh and forceful."

The style, however silly on occasion, gave the magazine a distinctive voice. Men were not famous but "famed," not powerful but "potent." High on the list of accolades was "able." All were masculine terms of approbation: the news in Homeric mode, demigods or villains on tiptoe. TIME's writers loved Homer's narrative techniques. Compound adjectives: Mexico's President Francisco Madero was "wild-eyed," while World War I German Admiral Alfred von Tirpitz was "long-whiskered." Public figures were tagged with mock-heroic identifying phrases. Minnesota's Senator Henrik Shipstead was invariably "the duck-hunting dentist."

1949 Circulation swelled as ex-G.I.s who read TIME during the war now subscribed on their own

An impasto of alliterative adjectives got slathered onto public men. George Bernard Shaw was "mocking, mordant, misanthropic." General Erich von Ludendorff was "flagitious, inscrutable, unrelenting." The intent was novelistic. As Luce explained it, "No idea exists outside a human skull—and no human skull exists without hair and a face and a voice—in fact the flesh and blood attributes of a human personality. TIME journalism began by being deeply interested in people, as individuals who were making history, or a small part of it, from week to week. We tried to make our readers see and hear and even smell these people as part of a better understanding of their ideas—or lack of them."

ALL THE WHILE FLOURISHED A CLASSICAL INVERSION OF sentences. An early writer, possibly suffering from a hangover, took the technique over the top with this effort: "A ghastly ghoul prowled around a cemetery not far from Paris. Into family chapels went he, robbery of the dead intent upon." But in 1936, TIMEstyle began to suffer bouts of self-consciousness. That was the year that the *New Yorker*, edited by an old nemesis of Luce's, Harold Ross, published Wolcott Gibbs' hilarious and devastating parody of TIME. "Backward ran sentences until reeled the mind," Gibbs wrote. He described Luce as an "ambitious, gimlet-eyed Baby Tycoon ... efficient, humorless ... brusque, contradictory, hostile." Luce was annoyed. At Rollins College, where he went to speak a few years later, he discovered that students in a class in contemporary biography were discussing him—and using as their text "that goddam article in the *New Yorker* ... Is this thing going to be engraved on my tombstone?"

Luce and Hadden put together the TIME prospectus in an upstairs office on East 17th Street in Manhattan. Soon, with a staff of 33, the magazine moved its offices to a loft building on 39th Street, former home of a brewery. In 1925, when Hadden took a European vacation, Luce indulged his wistfulness for heartland America (the instinct of a missionary's China-born child) and arranged to move the magazine to Cleveland, Ohio. The experiment mortified the pub-crawling and cosmopolitan Hadden, who waited until Luce went abroad two years later to organize a countermove, shipping everyone back to New York City.

When TIME began, its few writers assembled their material from newspaper clippings and a few reference books. In 1929 the first correspondent, David Hulburd, opened a bureau in Chicago, and a network of stringers—part-time, free-lance reporters—was organized to report from cities in the U.S. and Canada. During the '30s and early '40s, as the news turned urgent and global, TIME expanded its network into what eventually became the Time-Life News Service. By 1958 the magazine had 435 correspondents, stringers and writers reporting from 33 locations around the world. With advances in communications technology, those numbers have since been reduced, but a network of bureaus remains the core of the magazine's newsgathering system.

The TIME editorial process, evolved over a period of years, had the unique collective concentration (and for years, the anonymity) of a well-run beehive. Correspondents went forth into the fields collecting pollen (data, interviews, "bioperse"—or life stories with anecdotes and color) and sent it back to the New York hive by wire in long reports (files)—an immense redundancy of information that writers in New York boiled and kneaded and licked into stories for the magazine.

Senior editors then set to work. Some—like Laird Goldsborough, Foreign News editor in the '30s, or Whittaker Chambers, when he held the same post in the '40s—were famous around the magazine for rewriting almost every word of copy, using the writer's version merely as a guide for straight lines upon which to pencil the interlinear substitute. When the senior editor had initialed the copy, his version, retyped, went to the managing editor, whose mind was the needle's eye through which the entire magazine passed each week before going to press in Chicago.

1957 Twenty months before taking over Cuba, Fidel Castro reads TIME in his jungle hideout

After he formally ascended to the higher altitude of editor-in-chief in 1944, Luce continued to monitor major stories, reading them in advance before they appeared in the magazine. Following publication, he gave each edition of TIME a thorough and sometimes brutal cover-to-cover read, marking each story with words of criticism or praise. Hedley Donovan, the Minnesota-born Time Inc. veteran and former FORTUNE managing editor who succeeded Luce as editor-in-chief in 1964, followed the practice. So, with variations, have his successors Henry Grunwald, Jason McManus and Norman Pearlstine.

It was a grueling process of editorial refinement that either improved and sharpened the story at each successive stage, or distorted it as it passed from hand to hand and mind to mind. Sometimes correspondents in the field and editors in New York took exactly opposite views about whether a story had gone from bad to good or good to bad in the editorial alchemy.

1983 British Prime Minister Margaret Thatcher, a frequent cover subject, strikes a pose at an exhibit of TIME cover art

During Vietnam, a rift over editorial policy—the magazine's Saigon bureau's quarreling with the New York office's optimism about the war—eventually brought about a significant procedural change at TIME. Edited stories were thenceforth wired back to the reporting correspondents, whose comments and corrections were factored in before the stories went to press.

In the Luce tradition, however, TIME remained very much an editor's magazine. While researchers—and as of the '70s, correspondents—were the guardians of the magazine's factuality, the managing editor retained enormous authority through the selection of stories and, as TIME gradually introduced more personal opinion through bylined articles, the choice of writers.

The most public demonstration of editorial authority has been the annual selection of TIME's Man of the Year, a brilliant stroke of news packaging that Luce and Hadden invented during a no-news week late in 1927. Having neglected to put Charles A. Lindbergh on the cover the previous May, when he had made his famous solo flight, they concocted the Man of the Year idea to justify putting him on at year's end. The choice thereafter became a national guessing game, popular with advertisers but also a serious intellectual drill—a way to encourage Americans to think about the world, and the year just past, in the same ruthlessly appraising way Luce did.

Until the mid-'60s, the vast majority of TIME covers (99%) depicted people—Presidents, dictators, industrialists, generals, scientists, artists, writers, saints, revolutionaries—all in keeping with Luce's enthusiasm for flesh-and-blood personalities and his general sympathy with Carlyle's idea that great men cause great events. But with the '60s' challenge to

1998 Mikhail Gorbachev poses with his Man of the Decade cover at TIME's 75th-anniversary party

authority in almost every American institution, from the White House to the family, and the nation's effort to redefine its idea of social justice, TIME began to examine issues and ideas as often as it did personalities. The '60s' work of demystification tended to subvert the heroic, idealizing assumptions that TIME sometimes brought to its cover subjects. After Henry Grunwald became managing editor in 1968, succeeding Otto Fuerbringer, the trend toward cover stories about issues, ideas and events grew more pronounced. Instead of a Man or Woman of the Year for 1982, TIME designated the computer as Machine of the Year; for 1988 "Endangered Earth" was Planet of the Year.

In its 75 years, TIME has proved to be an adaptive organism, reinventing itself periodically. The red border on the cover, first used in 1927, and the familiar lettering of the logo have made the magazine unmistakable, giving it instant identity and reassuring familiarity. Inside the framework, TIME has added sections (Essay, Behavior, Notebook) and dropped sections (Crime, Animals, Aeronautics), gone from postage-stamp head shots in its early news columns to full-page color displays in which photography and imaginative graphics play a larger part. Amid the proliferation of other sources—including all-news radio and television, national editions of daily newspapers and now the Internet—the magazine has evolved into a mix of news and features that play off the news instead of simply recapping it. The Essay section and signed columns have added stronger, more personal voices to the magazine. Cultural criticism and essays began carrying bylines in 1970; other sections adopted bylines in 1980. The omniscient voice of group journalism has given way to scores of distinctive voices of writers who report and reporters who write what they have seen for themselves.

Today's TIME continues to evolve, as living things do. Yet if Briton Hadden and Henry Luce were still around, they'd certainly recognize their progeny. It would be interesting to give them a peek at a 1998 issue of the magazine—and ask them what they think of their work in progress. ∎

Alan Brinkley

TO SEE AND KNOW EVERYTHING

Henry R. Luce had insatiable curiosity, drive and ambition

conventional success of whatever magnitude. He had higher, perhaps unattainable, aims that he had absorbed in his youth and retained until his death.

Luce was born in 1898 in Tengchow (now P'eng-lai), China, where his father—a Presbyterian minister and missionary—headed a small college for Chinese converts to Christianity. Harry spent his entire childhood in China, except for one or two trips to visit relatives in the U.S. Like most missionary families, the Luces lived not among the Chinese but inside walled compounds, alongside other American and English clergy. The contrast between the ordered world of the missionary community and the harsh social and physical landscape outside it reinforced the assumptions driving the missionary project in China: the unquestioned belief in the moral superiority of Christianity and the cultural superiority of America; and the commitment to show the way not just to the love of Christ but also to a modern, scientific social order. The image of America that Luce had as a child was the idealized one his father and other missionaries created to justify their work. It was an image Luce never wholly abandoned.

Luce emerged from his youth with a deep sense of moral certainty matched by his unquenchable ambition and limitless curiosity. At an early age he began to crave books of all kinds. And he developed an almost obsessive attraction to travel. In 1913, at 15, he journeyed alone through Europe for four months before returning to the U.S. for prep school. He was, he said, "a fanatical sightseer," and he visited cities, museums and other sites with a relentless and methodical efficiency. That thirst for knowledge and experience—at times, it seemed, an almost undifferentiated thirst, a quest to see and know about everything, large and small, important and arcane—helped determine the direction of his career.

Luce spent the next seven years ensconced in all-male, all-white, overwhelmingly Protestant institutions of the American upper class: first Hotchkiss, then Yale (where he joined that bastion of the Establishment, Skull and Bones). Luce was active in student journalism in both schools—and in the process formed an intimate relationship with Briton Hadden, the classmate, friend and frequent rival with whom he would found TIME. Having encountered America first as an abstraction, Luce encountered it after 1913 as a member of a self-proclaimed enlightened élite,

T
HROUGH MOST OF AN EVENTFUL AND EXTRAORDINARILY successful life, Henry Luce—the co-founder of TIME and its undisputed leader for nearly 40 years—was not a wholly contented man. He was unsuccessful in his marriages; intermittently estranged from members of his family; frequently dismayed by the directions in which his nation, and the world, were moving. But what most concerned him was the gap he always saw between his own actions and the high purposes against which he measured them. He achieved great power, wealth and fame, and he was by any measure one of the most influential figures in the nation. But Luce was not satisfied with

1901 Luce, the son of Presbyterian missionaries, was raised in China

among boys and young men trained from an early age to think of themselves as natural social leaders. Such men did not often choose journalism as a career. To most of them, it remained a slightly disreputable profession, attractive to people of less elevated backgrounds—what the press critic A.J. Liebling once called "a refuge for the vaguely talented." But when Luce and Hadden set out in 1923, three years out of Yale, to create a journalistic institution of their own—a new weekly newsmagazine that they had begun envisioning while still undergraduates—they did so not to break from the norms of the world they had known at Hotchkiss and Yale; they did so to bring those norms into journalism. They would not simply report the news; they would interpret it for those who did not have the time, the energy or the knowledge to interpret it for themselves. Luce especially had a sense of what would become the century's scarcest commodity. He named his magazine after it: TIME, and designed it to be digested in less than an hour.

Brit Hadden, who had grown up in Brooklyn and was, much more than Luce, a product of middle-class America, wanted TIME to be the witty, sophisticated, even cynical voice of his generation—something like a newsman's version of H.L. Mencken's popular magazine *The Smart Set*. But to Luce, TIME had a different purpose. It was to be a vehicle of moral and political instruction, a point of connection between the world of élite ideas and opinion and middle-class people in the "true" America hungry for knowledge.

In 1929 Hadden died unexpectedly of a blood infection and Luce, though stunned, took the magazine in his strong hands. From then on, Time Inc. was his company and reflected his view of its mission—a view that intersected, much more successfully than Hadden's probably would have, with the character of the age. So prosperous did the company become that even during the Depression it could successfully launch two expensive new magazines—FORTUNE in 1930 and LIFE in 1936. By the end of World War II, Time Inc. was one of the largest and wealthiest publishing enterprises in the world.

The success fanned Luce's idealistic passions, and his commitments sometimes clouded his journalistic judgment. On the issues and people he cared most about—China, American foreign policy, the Republican Party, Chiang Kaishek, Winston Churchill, Wendell Willkie—he

1945 Luce and his son Hank in the South Pacific on the U.S.S. *Yorktown*

1952 Luce with Chiang Kai-shek, whose cause he fervently championed

1952 The perpetual traveler and wife Clare Boothe picnic in Spain

personally directed coverage at critical times with a feverish, occasionally suffocating intensity. And on those subjects his magazines could be startlingly biased, even polemical. On most issues, however, Luce was relatively open-minded, deferential to his editors, receptive to many conflicting views, eager to attract the talents of gifted writers whatever their ideologies. His own politics were, on the whole, only mildly and fairly flexibly conservative.

His personal life was far more difficult to balance. Luce had grown up in a kind of genteel poverty—a scholarship student working at menial jobs and pinching pennies among boys and young men of great wealth. Once he had a fortune, he lived in high style. He bought or built great houses, collected art, stayed only in the best suites in the best hotels. In 1935 he divorced his wife of 12 years (and the mother of his two sons) to marry one of the most glamorous women in America—the acclaimed editor and playwright, later Congresswoman and ambassador, Clare Boothe.

Their marriage was a troubled one from the start, a union of two ambitious, image-conscious people who did not always like each other very much and who were often apart. But they played their public roles as a dazzling and powerful couple to the hilt—entertaining lavishly (and deadly seriously), moving easily among the great and powerful, achieving celebrity and influence of a sort few publishers or journalists had ever known. To Harry, living an opulent and glamorous life was never satisfying in itself. At times, he confided to close friends, he considered it almost sinful.

As he neared the end of his career in the mid-1960s and began restlessly preparing for retirement, his great achievements—of which he was deeply proud—still seemed not wholly to satisfy him. He spent his last years in a search for the spiritual and emotional fulfillment he felt he had never fully achieved—a search so intense that he and Clare reportedly experimented with LSD, on the advice of friends who described it as a vehicle of awakening. At the end, in February 1967, when he died suddenly of a heart attack at age 68, he remained above all a missionary's son, still seeking the mission that would somehow fulfill and justify his rich, full, successful but never quite complete life. ∎

ALAN BRINKLEY is a professor of history at Columbia University who is writing a new biography of Henry Luce.

HOW TO CELEBRATE the anniversary of a magazine whose cover has featured the most significant people of the century? Well, why not invite every living cover subject to join us for a toast? That's how TIME observed its 40th anniversary in 1963—and in 1998, we turned around and did it again, at New York City's Radio City Music Hall.

Anniversary Party

HERE'S TO 75 MORE!

When TIME *throws a bash, VIPs RSVP*

CHEERS! Actress Sharon Stone toasts feminist pioneer Betty Friedan, left. The seats at Radio City were covered with a platform where the guests dined—before dancing on the stage

BOX-OFFICE CHAMP VS. BOXING CHAMP: The party was notable for its unusual mingling of celebrities from every sphere—including this matchup between Hollywood heavyweight Steven Spielberg and boxing superstar Evander Holyfield

1963: Gina Lollabrigida joins founder Henry Luce at TIME's 40th-birthday bash

THE FIRST OFFICES (1922)
TIME's prototype was designed in an upstairs office at this building on East 17th Street in Manhattan

THE FIRST IDEA (1918)
Fellow Yalies Henry Luce and Briton Hadden came up with the concept for a newsmagazine while in the Army

THE FIRST SUBSCRIBER (1922)
Judge Robert L. Luce, a distant cousin of Henry Luce's, sent in his check a year before publication. He was one of some 6,000 initial subscribers

WORKING THE ROOM: Henry Kissinger greets Mikhail and Raisa Gorbachev

WINNING SMILES: Nobel laureates Elie Wiesel and Toni Morrison; she toasted Martin Luther King

SPACE ACES: Actor Tom Hanks and veteran TV newsman Walter Cronkite swapped stories about the early days of NASA

SHE LOVES LUCY: In one of a series of tributes to influential people of the century, Mary Tyler Moore toasts her TV predecessor, Lucille Ball

HAIL TO THE CHIEFS: The Clintons join TIME president Bruce Hallett, managing editor Walter Isaacson and Time Warner head Gerald Levin

THE FIRST ISSUE (1923)

Dated March 3, 1923. The cover subject was Speaker of the House Joseph G. ("Uncle Joe") Cannon. The initial cover story was but a single column long

THE FIRST LETTERS TO THE EDITOR (1923)

"Bully," said one. "I am ready to acknowledge some measure of genius in this new conception of journalism," said another

THE FIRST COLOR FEATURE (1934)

Grant Wood's *American Gothic* was included in a section on the best U.S. artists

TIME IN THE TOONS

Both were born in the exuberant '20s, but TIME *is two years older than the* New Yorker—*and the upstart's cartoonists love to skewer our style*

KUDOS TO SOCIALITE NUDANCER

TIME has long had an inventive way with the English language

TIME COINAGES THAT CAUGHT ON:

socialite	male chauvinist
guesstimate	op art
World War II	televangelist

AND ONES THAT DIDN'T:

cinemoppet	cinemactor
legitimactor	radiorator
nudancer	Broadwayfarer
sexational	twinsult
politricks	newshawk

PREVIOUSLY ARCANE WORDS POPULARIZED BY TIME:

tycoon From Japanese: "great ruler"

pundit From Hindi: "learned man"

kudos From the Greek for "hear," as in acclamation—i.e., "hear, hear"

smog Combining "smoke" and "fog"; first used in San Francisco in 1905

"But, Lester, is it enough just being against everything that 'Time' magazine is for?"

McCALLISTER

A BERLITZ FOR SQUARES

Readers baffled by hipster lingo, whether spoken by Hollywood tough guys or Haight-Ashbury hippies, know they can count on TIME *for a translation*

"A 'beard,' in Hollywood parlance, is a man employed by a male star to accompany him when he appears in public with a woman not his wife. Sometimes female stars use them too. A 'hunker' is somebody kept on the payroll to know baseball scores, send out for coffee and strike matches on."

—*Aug. 29, 1955, from a footnote to a cover story on Frank Sinatra*

THE FIRST CHEESECAKE COVER (1936)

Leni Riefenstahl, the leading film director of the Third Reich (*Triumph of the Will*), showed off her skills as a Nordic skier for TIME readers

THE FIRST REPORTER KILLED ON THE JOB (1942)

Correspondent Melville Jacoby was hit by a plane on a runway in Australia during World War II. Since then, six other TIME journalists have been killed in the line of duty

THE FIRST FEMALE SENIOR EDITOR (1942)

Senior editor Mary Fraser was also chief of research. Up until the '60s, TIME's editors were almost exclusively male, the research staff female. Dress codes mandated stockings year-round

"That'll be the day!"

"Genial, outgoing Gil Wheat, I guess you know everybody: quiet, mild-mannered John Lilienthal; mordant, sardonic Geoff Relf; compact, dynamic Jim Stockton; serious, high-minded Art Herzog; brilliant, mercurial John Motheral; and me, of course—long-winded, boring Stan Norton."

"Jazz has unhappily splintered into hostile camps, musically and racially. The spirit and sound of each variety of jazz is carefully analyzed, isolated and pronounced a 'bag.' Within each bag, imitation of the 'daddy' spreads through the ranks like summer fires."

—Feb. 28, 1964, from a cover story on Thelonious Monk

"Hirsute, shoeless hippies huddled in doorways, smoking pot, 'rapping' (achieving rapport with random talk), or banging beer cans in time to ubiquitous jukebox rhythms. They scorn money—they call it 'bread.' They feel 'uptight' (tense and frightened) about many disparate things—from sex to the draft, college grades to thermonuclear war."

—July 7, 1967, from a cover story on San Francisco's hippies

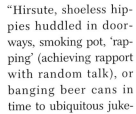

"Coke paraphernalia are openly displayed in 'head shops' like Washington's Pleasure Chest. The process of spreading the coke on a table in 'lines' for sniffing is as elaborate and careful as a Japanese tea ceremony. Since sniffing cocaine produces such a quick, short boost, more and more users have sought the deeper ecstatic 'rush' that comes from 'freebasing,' smoking a chemically treated form of the powder."

—July 6, 1981, from a cover story on cocaine culture

THE FIRST EDITORIAL (1973)

At the height of the Watergate scandal, TIME urged President Nixon to resign. The unsigned piece was written by managing editor Henry Grunwald

THE FIRST GIVEAWAY TO SUBSCRIBERS (1976)

It was the story of the week America declared Independence (as if reported by TIME in 1776)

THE FIRST INTERNET SPIN-OFF (1993)

TIME's appearance on America Online was followed by the creation of our own Website in 1994

OLD NEWS IS EXPENSIVE NEWS

Have any yellowing copies of TIME lying around? They might actually be worth something. "Over the past two years," says New York City magazine dealer Mike Gallagher, "TIME has really broken out. It's more collectible now than LIFE—and scarcer." The most valuable issues (largely based on cover subject, with athletes, entertainers and Nazis especially prized):

COVER SUBJECT AND DATE	VALUE
Joseph G. Cannon (first issue), March 23, 1923	$1,000
Al Capone March 23, 1930	$500
Bobby Jones Aug. 31, 1925	$500
Joe DiMaggio July 13, 1936	$500
Jimmy Foxx July 29, 1929	$300
The Marx Brothers Aug. 15, 1932	$300
Connie Mack April 11, 1927	$250
Frank Lloyd Wright Jan. 17, 1938	$200
Charles Lindbergh Man of the Year, Jan. 2, 1928	$200
Bruce Springsteen Oct. 27, 1975	$200
Rogers Hornsby July 9, 1928	$200
Dizzy Dean April 15, 1935	$200
Vivien Leigh as Scarlett O'Hara Dec. 25, 1939	$200
Marilyn Monroe May 14, 1956	$200

Ten issues are valued at $150, including covers featuring Sigmund Freud, Charlie Chaplin, George Gershwin and 1938 Man of the Year Adolf Hitler

THE REVIEWS ARE IN

Just as TIME *commented on the world, so did the world comment on* TIME. *In some cases, depending on the source, brickbats may have been welcomed*

"Prosy was the first issue of TIME on March 3, 1923. Yet to suggest itself as a rational method of communication, of infuriating readers into buying the magazine, was strange inverted TIMEstyle. It was months before [editor Briton] Hadden's impish contempt for his readers, his impatience with the English language, crystallized into gibberish. By the end of the first year, however, TIMEeditors were calling people able, potent, nimble. 'Great word! Great word!' would crow Hadden, coming upon 'snaggle-toothed,' 'pig-faced.' Appearing also were first gratuitous invasions of privacy. Stressed was the bastardy of Ramsay MacDonald, the 'cozy hospitality' of Mae West. Backwards ran sentences until reeled the mind."
—*Wolcott Gibbs, profiling Henry Luce in* TIMEstyle *in the* New Yorker, *1936*

"TIME made its debut not long after *Ulysses.* The prim, as well as the encyclopedic, arrogance of Stephen Daedalus offered an easily adaptable pose for the restless young journalist. In a word, TIME, LIFE, and FORTUNE are the American Bloomsbury, our psychological bureaucracy, inhabited by well-paid artist-apes. The 'sophisticated' tone of TIME, then, arises from nothing more than queasiness about the main march of the human affections, which issues as hard-boiled flippancy. And it is the whole world, of course, which is dear dirty Dublin to the omnivorous hackmen of *T.L.F.*"
—*Marshall McLuhan in the journal* Neurotica, *1949*

"Oh, Mr. Screwluce! Timidity will never win back your mag's deserters and their splendid coin. Milquetoasting will get people to thinking that your reformed Communist (recent TIME chief editor Whittaker Chambers) represented ALL your editorial guts."
—*Walter Winchell, column, 1949*

"TIME was conceived as a moral, civic, and literary experience of a normative kind. About a special country. For all that the writing style of TIME was often mannered, it reflected the work of editorial talents from Middle America, so that if [it] sometimes seemed supercilious, the reader was getting the high wit and lusty talent of utterly indigenous Americans arguing the conventional virtues."
—*William F. Buckley Jr., in* Esquire, *1983*

PARALLEL UNIVERSE

For many years, TIME's editors prepared two cover treatments before each election, ensuring a quick turnaround once the results were in. New technology makes that unnecessary now—but we miss these relics of an alternate history

BARRY GOLDWATER, 1964 The late Senator won only 39% of the vote

HUBERT HUMPHREY, 1968 The closest call. Humphrey lost by only 0.7%

WALTER MONDALE 1984 As expected (note the cover line), Mondale got 41% of the vote

HITS

The 10 most popular issues of TIME at the newsstand

ISSUE DATE	COVER SUBJECT	NO. OF COPIES SOLD
Sept. 15, 1997	PRINCESS DIANA "COMMEMORATIVE"	1,183,758
Sept. 8, 1997	DEATH OF PRINCESS DIANA	802,838
Aug. 19, 1974	PRESIDENT NIXON'S RESIGNATION	564,723
Dec. 22, 1980	DEATH OF JOHN LENNON	531,340
March 19, 1984	MICHAEL JACKSON	500,290
Aug. 2, 1982	HERPES	468,021
Feb. 10, 1986	*CHALLENGER* EXPLOSION	462,492
Jan. 28, 1991	WAR IN THE GULF	433,625
Aug. 15, 1983	BABIES: "WHAT DO THEY KNOW?"	423,156
June 2, 1980	MOUNT ST. HELENS	412,909

MISSES

The 10 least popular issues of TIME at the newsstand (since 1980)

ISSUE DATE	COVER SUBJECT	NO. OF COPIES SOLD
Oct. 10, 1994	BLACK CULTURAL RENAISSANCE	100,827
Aug. 22, 1994	BASEBALL STRIKE	101,125
May 17, 1993	"ANGUISH OVER BOSNIA"	102,193
April 4, 1996	NUCLEAR SAFETY	108,900
June 10, 1996	BENJAMIN NETANYAHU	109,300
March 29, 1993	BORIS YELTSIN	109,365
Dec. 21, 1992	SOMALIA: RESTORING HOPE	111,176
June 3, 1996	ADVOCATES FOR CHILDREN	111,700
Nov. 20, 1995	G.O.P. FRONT RUNNER BOB DOLE	112,310
Oct. 24, 1994	AMERICA'S ECONOMY	113,041

"DEAR IDIOTS..."

Below are the 10 cover stories that generated the heaviest reader mail—typically, most of it angry. The top four also provoked the most subscription cancellations

YEAR	COVER SUBJECT	NO. OF LETTERS
1980	Ayatullah Khomeini, Man of the Year	14,081
1973	*Last Tango in Paris*	12,191
1966	Is God Dead?	3,500
1964	Sex in the U.S.	3,336
1989	Death by Gun (everyone killed in one week in the U.S.)	2,361
1996	Newt Gingrich, Man of the Year	2,283
1998	Monica Lewinsky and Bill Clinton	2,199
1963	Assassination of J.F.K./ New President L.B.J.	2,182
1988	Who Was Jesus?	2,121
1997	Ellen DeGeneres	2,085

Khomeini: Not the people's choice

SPITTIN' IMAGES

Its popularity, its longevity—and that instantly familiar red border—have made TIME a favorite target of parodists over the years. Kudos to the wags at the Harvard *Lampoon,* three of whose rollicking rip-offs are shown here

1965 A faraway land, Vietnam, was still a subject for humor, not anguish

1969 Having it both ways, this cover "parodies" using cheesecake to boost sales

1989 Dead ringers for the Bushes make this sassy cover hoax work

EXUBERANCE

In the aftermath of
the Great War,
America discovered
an ebullient culture
and an ambitious,
courageous spirit

FLYING FEET
Fueled by prohibited alcohol,
Americans shed their inhibitions
and kicked up their heels

SOARING DREAMS

Charles Lindbergh, preparing for his flight to Paris, personified the American zest for adventure

EXUBERANCE 1923-1929

Robert Hughes

A PASSION FOR THE NEW

In the jazz age, America discovered its cultural voice

I T'S NO EXAGGERATION TO SAY THAT THE 1920S FORMED MODERN AMERICA IN WAYS SO vast and far-reaching that we take them for granted today—particularly in the field of culture but no less in America's consciousness of itself as a society and of the place it might have in the world. World War I had destroyed the Old Order in Europe and made a superpower of democratic, industrial America. It seemed obvious to many Americans that they were poised, collectively, to lead the world. And the future American, wrote a Jewish dramatist named Israel Zangwill in a play famously titled *The Melting Pot,* would be the supreme alloy of obstructive difference: "the fusion of all races, perhaps the coming superman."

In the '20s, American painters, sculptors and architects still defined themselves largely in terms of European models, whether of "traditional" art or of Modernism. But the decade also saw the emergence of a genius of American design who was perhaps the greatest architect of the century: Frank Lloyd Wright. The decade's supreme collective artifact, in steel and stone, was, of course, Manhattan itself, with its immense towers—Chrysler, Empire State and the rest—rising like blasts of congealed and shining energy from the bedrock, a spectacle of Promethean ambition and daring.

Institutional novelty was the American way, and the '20s created institutions that would have seemed contradictions in terms in Paris or London: a Museum of Modern Art, for instance, which opened in 1929. New York City was turning into an international culture, which would make it a natural haven for artists and intellectuals displaced by Nazism in the '30s—whose presence, in turn, would help make the city into Modernism's center of gravity in the '50s. New York was the world's "shock city," and would remain so for decades to come—not least because it harbored such cultural variety. Another sign of this was the Harlem Renaissance, permeated by America's greatest indigenous musical forms, jazz and the blues.

BUT THE BIGGEST CHANGE WAS THE RISE of American popular culture: not only jazz and its innumerable variants but also what happened onstage, across the airwaves and on the movie screen. America took the European operetta, fused it with burlesque and jazz and created—through the genius of Irving Berlin, Jerome Kern, Richard Rodgers and others—a broad, unique musical form. The '20s saw the rise of the Hollywood studio system, which had grown from its humble origins among (mostly immigrant Jewish) nickelodeon proprietors into the most powerful industry for the invention and spread of dreams in human history, at least until the advent of TV. Walt Disney invented a little mouse that would become a behemoth.

Americans discovered their insatiable hunger for the electronic, which would create huge communal audiences: 60,000 households had radio sets in 1922; more than 10 million had sets in 1929. The country began to turn itself into an image-saturated, stimulus-bombarded factory of desire. By the '70s and '80s, with the boom in electronic communications, U.S. popular and kitsch culture would dominate the globe as no other had, with no limit in sight. So it was in the '20s that America's cultural fantasies started to become, for good or ill, the world's. ∎

K.K.K.
PROCESSION

Hiram Wesley Evans, Imperial Wizard, resplendent in purple and gold, smiled and bowed hat in hand as he proudly led some 30,000 to 50,000 Klansmen and Klanswomen down Pennsylvania Avenue from the Capitol to the Treasury. Occasionally the crowds along the way applauded, but there was neither cheering nor jeering ... Most of the demonstrators were from the North. Texas had barely 200 in line. Georgia, Louisiana, South Carolina, Alabama, Tennessee, Mississippi apparently were not represented. Pittsburgh alone had 2,000 marchers.   **AUG. 17, 1925**

INDIANS
THE VISITOR

To his haughty redskin brothers, to the haughty strong Sioux nation, with his wife and son beside him, with big medicine in his pocket, came the pale Wamblee-Tokaha (Leading Eagle) New White Chief and High Protector—otherwise, Calvin Coolidge, 29th U.S. President, but first ever to visit any Amerindians on one of the reservations set aside for them by their Caucasian conquerors. He came and was received in peace and friendship.   **AUG. 29, 1927**

PROHIBITION

"NOT GUILTY"

John Philip Hill of Baltimore, recently indicted for violating the Volstead Act, was tried last week. And John Philip Hill was acquitted. John Philip is a character. In the sparkling words of Correspondent Clinton W. Gilbert: "Farmers could make cider and no one went around to find out how much alcohol it contained. Well, why not have a farm in a Baltimore backyard? He had two windows painted on his front fence with painted cows' heads looking out of them. Then he had apple trees with apples carefully tied on them moved into his back yard. Then he set up a cider press and allowed his cider to ferment just a bit, and he gave his neighbors to drink. He was indicted on six counts for illegal manufacture and possession of the forbidden."

NOV. 24, 1924

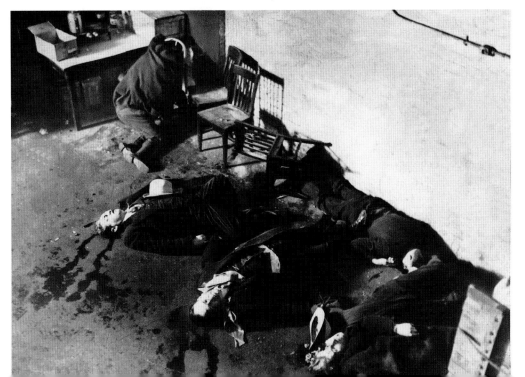

CRIME

CHICAGO STYLE

It was 10:20 o'clock on St. Valentine's morning. Chicago brimmed with sentiment and sunshine. Peaceful was even the booze-peddling depot, masked as a garage, where lolled six underworldlings ... Through the door strode four men. Two, in police uniforms, swung sub-machine guns. Two, in plain clothes, carried stubby shotguns ... Tin coffee cups clattered to the floor. Snarled orders lined the six gangsters up against the wall. The garage became a thunder-box of explosions.   **FEB. 25, 1929**

ITALY

NARY A SCRATCH

When a group of admirers presented Mussolini with a lioness cub they supposed he would scarcely venture to play with her after a few months. To the despair of his guards Signor Mussolini has become so attached to the now full-grown lioness that he insists on entering her cage for an occasional frolic ... When he calls: "Italia Bella!" the lithe, tawny beast bounds up to him. To date Il Duce has suffered barely a scratch from her claws. Like her namesake, "Fair Italy," she appears to adore him.   **JULY 12, 1926**

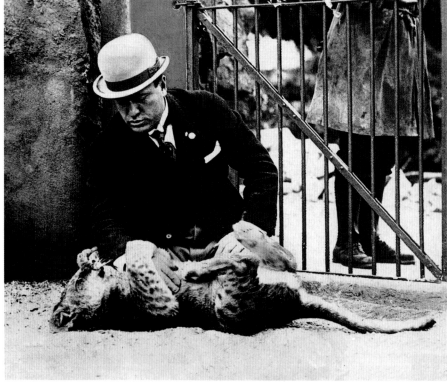

COMMONWEALTH

WINNIE'S DEFEAT

Otho Nicholson had won by a majority of 43 votes. Churchill turned ashen pale. His cigar dropped from his mouth and rolled unnoticed to the floor. His wife buried her face in her hands. "Demand a recount," whispered his campaign manager. "I demand a recount!" cried "Winnie." The result was the same.   **MARCH 31, 1924**

GERMANY

AN ACQUITTAL

There came an end to the treason trial at Munich. Feldmarschall Erich von Ludendorff (flagitious, inscrutable, unrelenting) was acquitted of all blame for his part in the so-called "Beer Hall" uprising of last Fall.

The General appeared for his final day in court equipped in full military regalia with numerous orders, decorations ... Adolf Hitler, the other prime instigator of the revolt, was sentenced to five years of confinement in a fortress and fined 200 gold marks. Since it was understood that Hitler will be obliged to serve only six months—and then receive a parole ... his followers received the verdict with loud approval, deluged [the pair] with floral tributes.   **APRIL 7, 1924**

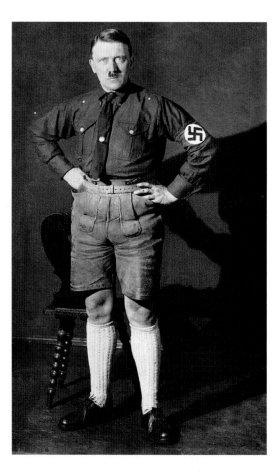

"SOUL THRUST"

[Indians] talk not of howitzers nor of horse power but rather of how to evoke from teeming millions a cumulative "soul thrust" which shall rock the world. One and all they defer to the *Mahatma:* "the Great Soul," Mohandas K. Gandhi … last week he squatted upon his usual dais, naked except for his habitual skimpy loin cloth, emaciated from much fasting and prayer, and wearing as his sole adornment a cheap nickel-plated watch suspended from his neck.   **JAN. 9, 1928**

COLD DEATH

Nikolai Lenin died Monday, Jan. 21. On the following Sunday at 4 p.m. he was buried in Moscow. In the interval "the greatest number of people who had ever looked upon the same corpse" (exact number unspecified) passed before his body which lay in state. All of them had stood in line in the streets of Moscow for 10, 20, 30 hours, in inhuman cold … A blizzard raged. Sparrows fell frozen in the streets. Ice covered the horses of the guards. Three gigantic bonfires in Red Square melted the ice for the burial.   **FEB. 4, 1924**

LAW

CLARENCE DARROW

To a greater extent than that of any other lawyer in the history of American jurisprudence, the professional life of Clarence S. Darrow has consisted in defending men standing in the shadow of the gallows with the hostile eyes of the country upon them. (Mr. Darrow, as everyone knows, is chief counsel for the Leopold-Loeb defense.) ... Darrow has been frequently characterized in the press as "a great stage artist, a greater artist than lawyer." One M.L. Edgar, in the St. Louis *Mirror*, has described his personal appearance thus: "His face is shot through with lines, lines which he will never permit a photographer to erase because, as he says, 'it cost me too much to get them.'" **AUG. 18, 1924**

SCIENCE

BEHOLD THE KING

To his Egyptian Majesty, King Tut-ankh-Amen, death came about 3,300 years ago, after 17 years of life, eight of matrimony, three or four of sovereignty. King Tut was a slim lad, slender, saplingesque. Nothing so became him as his burial. The reconstruction of his magnificent interment was accomplished last week by Howard Carter and colleagues in the Valley of the Kings at Luxor. After three years of laborious archaeology, the diggers opened the royal coffin for the first time. **NOV. 30, 1925**

A MONTH OF SUNDAY

Leaping and snarling like a small, vivacious cougar, Rev. William A. Sunday preached at the Coliseum in St. Louis. It was the fifth week of the projected seven-week revival meeting; Billy Sunday had signed up about 4,000 converts and he wanted some more. He talked about the opera *Faust*, in which Marguerite, a pregnant girl, dies of broken-heart. Said Billy Sunday: "How would this dame feel, this dame in the box, with the accordion chin, all dressed up in silk and diamonds, if she found her path obstructed by a real Marguerite? She can shed crocodile tears over the false Marguerite on stage—shed some real tears over the real ones, you big fraud!" **FEB. 27, 1928**

MAN OF THE YEAR 1927–1929

WHILE IT WOULD BE PLEASING TO CLAIM THAT TIME's famous annual designation of a Man or Woman of the Year was the product of careful planning, the truth is more mundane—and more revealing. Faced with a slow news week at the end of 1927, the editors were casting about for a cover subject. Recalling that TIME had failed to put Charles Lindbergh on the cover after his transatlantic flight, someone suggested a Lindbergh cover titled "Man of the Year." The week's dilemma was solved, and a tradition was born. ■

1927 Since TIME's first Man of the Year, **Charles Lindbergh,** was a popular hero, many readers thought the designation was an honor. But the choice reflects one's influence on the news for good or ill—as shown by the selection of Adolf Hitler in 1938.

1928 Walter Chrysler rocked Detroit by buying Dodge and unveiling a new line, the Plymouth.

1929 U.S. businessman **Owen D. Young** chaired the second post-war Reparations Conference.

THEATER
RATTLE-BRAINED REVELRY

No musical show this season has excited more blissful anticipation than this return of the Marx Brothers. These four ingenious gentlemen first sprang into magnificent prominence two years ago with the noisy, nondescript and stunningly hilarious show *I'll Say She Is. The Cocoanuts* [offers] scene after scene of rattle-brained revelry. Groucho (with the cigar) and Harpo (he says nothing) are the principal disturbances. **DEC. 21, 1925**

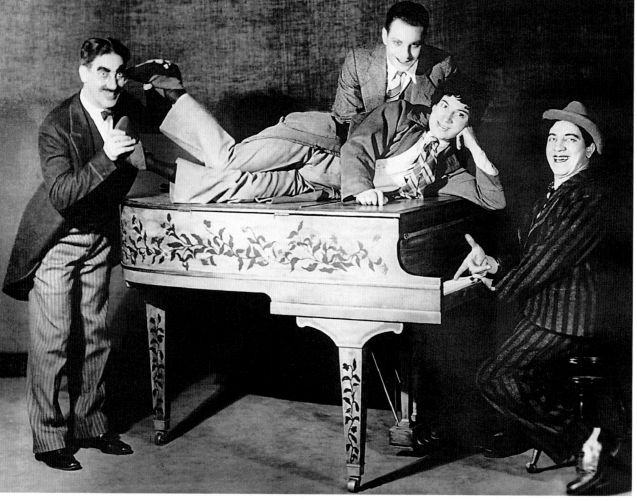

ART
MONET'S EYES

Claude Monet, Prince of Impressionists, earlier reported to have recovered his sight, went under the surgeon's knife for the third time at his home at Giverny … When the bandage was removed, M. Monet could see clearly with one eye, but further surgery may be necessary. The great age of the painter (81) adds danger to the delicate task. Monet still hopes to complete the great mural design of water lilies upon which he was working when blindness fell upon him. **AUG. 6, 1923**

MUSIC
ONLY SIX

The guitar has never been an exalted instrument, has never made great history in music. Its living has been a meagre one, eked out on the vaudeville stage, thwanging accompaniments to this ditty and that. Last week in Manhattan, for the first time in memory, it braved a formal recital.

There was nothing extraordinary about the recital guitar. It had just six strings. Andrès Segovia, the Spaniard who brought it to the U.S., had just the allotted ten fingers but he made big music ... Even a suite of the great J.S. Bach was played with amazing virtuosity and an infinite variety of tonal color. **JAN. 16, 1928**

CINEMA
BUSTER

The Navigator. Buster Keaton is like President Coolidge. You either like him or you do not. If you are one of the latter, you will stay away from the box-office polls. Otherwise, you will watch him on shipboard, attacked by cannibals, prodded by swordfish. You will continue happily in his constituency. **OCT. 20, 1924**

BOOKS
MRS. WOOLF'S WAY

In *To the Lighthouse* Author Virginia Woolf's stream-of-consciousness technique is present as before but its presence is subtler, more diffused. Now, in her brilliant offensive on the human soul, she does not perpetrate an open advance. Weaving, stalking spying from thickets, she discovers the nature of her prey. The actual capture she leaves to those who, reading her book, are her companions in the chase. **MAY 30, 1927**

ARTS
NEW VOICES

1924 Eugene O'Neill made the first of his four TIME covers with *All God's Chillun Got Wings.*

1924 Broadway star **Ethel Barrymore** was one of the few women on the cover in the '20s.

1925 Amy Lowell: the author of "brilliant and brittle verse," she "uses psychology as a spade."

1925 Charlie Chaplin: "his hat, feet, waddle and smirk are familiar to South Sea Islanders."

THE DUELISTS AND THE DANSEUSE

Dawn revealed on a field of honor near Budapest last week two duelists, a Hungarian cavalry officer and an Italian count, who faced each other with sharp swords because of a U.S. danseuse from Harlem, famed **Josephine Baker** … the tawny, chocolate toast of jaded Parisian boulevardiers.   **MAY 28, 1928**

THE CHAMPION

William Harrison Dempsey has never been a popular champion … Furthermore, he is a lowbrow. His grammar is gummy at the edges; he makes no bones about his ignorance of philosophy. Pinochle is his favorite game, and he addresses his butler as "Babe."   **AUG. 30, 1926**

EINSTEIN'S WORLD

Dr. and Mrs. **Albert Einstein** are cousins. March 14 he will be 50 years old. She is almost that age. She is a level-headed, practical woman who finds her philosophizing husband no nuisance. Said she of him some time ago: "Professor Einstein is not eccentric. He wears stiff collars when the occasion demands it without protest. He hardly ever mislays things. At least, not more than most men. He knows when it's time for lunch and dinner."   **FEB. 18, 1929**

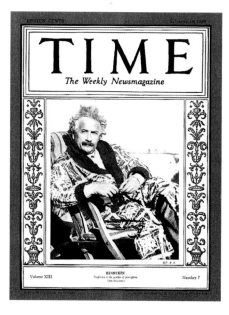

THE BANDIT KING

The jaunty, clean-limbed incumbent of the $30,000,000 Peacock Throne of Persia was once a swashbuckling bandit, Reza Khan. Now he is **Reza Shah Pahlevi,** King of Kings.   **APRIL 23, 1928**

FREUD AND FREUDISM

Among **Sigmund Freud's** pupils are such men as Adler, Jung, Stekel. It is important to note that Freud quarreled with each. Freud once referred to himself as "the only rogue in a company of immaculate rascals." Jung "has a proud stomach" and parted company with Freud. **OCT. 27, 1924**

THE INCORRIGIBLE IDEALIST

Now the world, tired of **George Bernard Shaw,** this giver of evil gifts, ready to kick him out of the age which, in spite of him, is so much like him, discovers that the old man has brought back to life a brave and beautiful creature—Joan of Arc. **DEC. 24, 1923**

OUSTED

An event every bit as amusing as it was surprising, was the eviction from the Forbidden City of **P'u-Yi,** Son of Heaven, Emperor of China. The 18-year-old Emperor's title and privileges are abolished ... Last year, on Dec. 1, 1923, he married and chose the name of Henry for himself. **NOV. 17, 1924**

TALKING BULLDOG

Knute Rockne, in his tenser moments, looks like an infuriated bulldog. Sometimes he talks that way. His talks to the team have made Notre Dame the best advertised football college in the land ... He has no secret of success; no formula. He knows what to do; tells his players, and they do it. **NOV. 7, 1927**

ON A ROLL

To a Germany laboring under the onus of World War I reparations and hyperinflation, Adolf Hitler brought a dynamic new energy and focus—at a terrible price

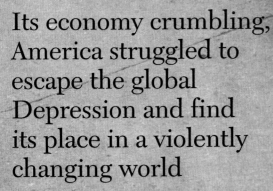

DESPAIR

Its economy crumbling,
America struggled to
escape the global
Depression and find
its place in a violently
changing world

George J. Church

TAKING CARE OF OUR OWN

The New Deal probed the limits of government

THE DOMINANT FIGURES OF THE 1930S CAME TO POWER ALMOST SIMULTANEOUSLY: Adolf Hitler on Jan. 30, 1933; Franklin D. Roosevelt 33 days later. It was no coincidence. Each embodied drive and vision—one diabolic, the other democratic—at the very moment their respective countries, and the world, had reached a nadir of economic and social despair. It had taken more than three years to plumb that bottom. Long after the 1929 stock-market crash filled Wall Street with eerily silent crowds gaping in stunned apprehension, President Herbert Hoover was still clinging to the deeply held—and widely shared—belief that good old rugged individualism, with just a dash of government help (nothing so radical as a federal dole), would dispel the growing Depression.

But the economy only spiraled lower. By 1933 unemployment had hit 25%; people were foraging in garbage dumps for food; outside almost every large city, shantytowns, known as "Hoovervilles," sheltered the newly homeless. On the eve of Roosevelt's Inauguration, a series of panicky runs on banks threatened to bring down the entire American financial system.

Roosevelt promised—and delivered—"action and action now." His New Deal was an amalgam of "alphabet" agencies (AAA, WPA, SEC, FDIC, NLRB, NRA) and work-relief projects that set the jobless to work building dams, bridges, highways and airports. Congress enacted such now hallowed (but then radical) reforms as Social Security, unemployment compensation and federal insurance of bank deposits.

For many, like the workers forming the National Recovery Administration's blue eagle symbol at right,

the New Deal was a blessing. To others, it spelled revolution, though except for the bloody battles fought by union organizers, strikers and company goons at some factory gates, it was a remarkably peaceful one. For the New Deal, after all, reflected another deeply held belief with roots in the nation's pioneer past: that Americans take care of their own. Though there were those who hated him, F.D.R. by 1936 had inspired enough public hope and confidence to win one of the most overwhelming electoral victories in U.S. history—which made him something of an anomaly. Outside the U.S. the 1930s was an era of dictatorship and, increasingly, of death. In the Soviet Union millions perished in the Ukraine famine of 1932-33 and the Great Terror of 1936-38. Hitler, meanwhile, was ending German unemployment largely by building a war machine that had to be turned loose eventually—and was, on Sept. 1, 1939.

PROBABLY MORE THAN ANY OF ROOSEVELT'S SOCIAL PROGRAMS, IT WAS THE WAR THAT FINALLY wrenched America free from the Depression. But the apparent success of the New Deal raised the softer, more charitable side of the national psyche to an ascendancy over reliance on rugged individualism. Big Government would later expand far beyond anything the New Dealers had ever imagined—first during World War II, then in Lyndon Johnson's Great Society. Republicans Dwight Eisenhower and Richard Nixon campaigned as philosophical opponents of Big Government, but once in power they made no real attempt to cut it back. Even Ronald Reagan could do little more than put a lid on its expansion. It took Democrat Bill Clinton to declare the era of Big Government finally over. And by then its most important institutions had become widely accepted provisions of the nation's contract with itself. ■

BUSINESS & FINANCE

PANIC

For so many months so many people had saved money and borrowed money and borrowed on their borrowings to possess themselves of the little pieces of paper by virtue of which they became partners in U.S. Industry. Now they were trying to get rid of them even more frantically than they had tried to get them. Stocks bought without reference to their earnings were being sold without reference to their dividends. At around noon there came the no-bid menace ... stocks were dropping from 2 to 10 points between sales ... Sound stocks at shrunk prices—and nobody to buy them. It looked as if U.S. Industry's little partners were in a fair way to bankrupt the firm. **NOV. 4, 1929**

CONSERVATION

VALLEY OF VISION

With six pens and a happy smile President Roosevelt last week brought into being the Tennessee Valley Authority, another administrative engine for planned economy. Modeled after the Port of New York Authority, this independent Federal agency, with its own credit and its own crew, is to undertake what the President had called "the widest experiment ever conducted by a government"—the industrial development of a 640,000-sq.-mi. watershed. Its domain starts in the heights of the Cumberland Mountains, sweeps down past Knoxville, dips into Alabama, turns north through Tennessee and Kentucky and ends on the Ohio. In this vast basin the U.S. Government is not only going into business on a grand scale but is inviting U.S. Industry to join it in a project which may change the whole economic character of the central South. **MAY 29, 1933**

FEDERAL POWER: The TVA's Pickwick Landing Dam in Tennessee went into service in 1938

BATTLE OF THE REPUBLIC BARRIER

Greatest union bitterness was reserved for the struggle at Republic Steel's plant in South Chicago. A crowd of some 1,500 strikers tried to seize and close the plant, were stopped by 150 police. First it was clubs and tear gas versus clubs and numbers. The mob began hurling rocks and steel bolts, using slingshots with severe accuracy. The police faltered, then drew their guns and charged, firing first into the air, then at human targets. When the smoke and gas cleared five strikers lay dead or dying. **JUNE 7, 1937**

BLOWTORCH LYNCHINGS

In Winona, Miss., Roosevelt Townes and Bootjack McDaniels, 26-year-old Negroes, pleaded not guilty to a charge of murdering a crossroads country grocer ... But when they stepped out of a side door of the courthouse, they found themselves face to face with what so often handles cases like theirs in the South. An angry mob surged forward, took them from the custody of their guardians without a struggle ... Heavy chains clinked as the two blackamoors were made fast to trees. Bootjack McDaniels was asked to confess first. He gibbered that he was innocent. A mobster stepped forward with a plumber's blowtorch, lighted it. Again he refused to confess. Then the blue-white flame stabbed into his chest ... **APRIL 26, 1937**

S O V I E T   U N I O N

CAMPAIGN AGAINST RELIGION

Striking were events in the Kremlin's campaign against Religion last week; but more important is it to realize that every week, almost every day, some Russian church is being turned into a school, day nursery, workers' dormitory, theater, factory or a granary—as in the case of the once glorious House of God at Petrovsky, now rapidly filling with grain which will obliterate its lower tier of angels and finally its higher tier of adoring saints. The Cathedral of St. Isaac in Leningrad is now the Counter-Religion Museum. In Tiflis the 100-ton chimes of the Cathedral were recently melted down and sums raised by selling the metal were spent to establish the Tiflis Worker's Zoo.   **FEB. 3, 1930**

IN THE DRIVER'S SEAT

The figure of Adolf Hitler strode over a cringing Europe with all the swagger of a conqueror. Hitler became in 1938 the greatest threatening force that the democratic, freedom-loving world faces today. The Fascintern, with Hitler in the driver's seat, with Mussolini, Franco and the Japanese military cabal riding behind, emerged in 1938 as an international, revolutionary movement. Rant as he might against the machinations of international Communism and international Jewry … Führer Hitler had himself become the world's No. 1 International Revolutionist.

A generation ago western civilization had apparently outgrown the major evils of barbarism except for war between nations. The Russian Communist Revolution promoted the evil of class war. Hitler topped it by another, race war. Fascism and Communism both resurrected religious war. These multiple forms of barbarism gave shape in 1938 to an issue over which men may again, perhaps soon, shed blood: the issue of civilized liberty *v.* barbaric authoritarianism.   **JAN. 2, 1939**

CHIEF OF STATE

Adolf Hitler and Benito Mussolini have given Francisco Franco some valuable advice and object lessons on dealing with big powers like England and France. It remains doubtful whether the little mustached Generalissimo will ever come up to the calibre of his German and Italian mentors, but with further coaching from his Fascist friends, he may be able to hold on to his job for years. The friends hope so.   **MARCH 27, 1939**

41

SPORT

MASTER RACE?

That the Olympic Games afford harmless amusement to participants & spectators, a valuable chance for ballyhoo to the nation which holds them, no one is better aware than Realmleader Adolf Hitler, who attended every session except one in Berlin last week

By last week, the track & field events were finished. The No. 1 hero of the world's No. 1 sports event was a Cleveland Negro named Jesse Owens ... On the first day, coffee-colored Owens broke the world record for 100 metres in a trial heat. On the second day, he won the final in world-record time. On the third, he won the broad jump with a new Olympic record. On the fourth, he won the 200-metre dash ... then he helped the U.S. 400-metre relay team break the world's record in winning the final ...

Hitler conspicuously neglected to invite Negro winners up to shake hands with him in his box.   **AUG. 17, 1936**

THE FIRST LADY

UBIQUITOUS

Franklin Roosevelt's Eleanor uses No. 1600 Pennsylvania Ave. less as a home than as a base of operations. Since March 4 she has traveled incessantly up & down the nation, visiting all manner of places and institutions. She has traversed its skies and its surface so thoroughly that, in epitomizing her ubiquity for the ages, the *New Yorker* pictured two coalminers at work in the earth's bowels. One miner is saying: "For gosh sakes! Here comes Mrs. Roosevelt!"

NOV. 20, 1933

PAYOFF: In 1935—18 months after this story ran—Eleanor Roosevelt visited a coal mine

MAN OF THE YEAR 1930–1938

1930 His jailing by the British in India brought the world's attention to **Mohandas Gandhi.**

1931 Pierre Laval: his energy and vision restored France to the center of world events.

1932 As the nation faced economic calamity, **Franklin D. Roosevelt** was elected President.

1933 The National Recovery Administration's boss, **Hugh S. Johnson,** embodied the New Deal.

1934 "A cheerful, charming gentleman," **Franklin D. Roosevelt** battled the Depression.

1935 Ethiopia's King, **Haile Selassie,** fought an incursion by Italy's strongman, Mussolini.

1936 Wallis Simpson and her new husband, once King Edward VIII, shook the British crown.

1937 Japan's invasion of China imperiled "Man and Wife of the Year" **Gen. and Mme. Chiang.**

WITNESS — Ralph Ingersoll on Adolf Hitler as Man of the Year 1938

I was publisher at TIME, and the Man of the Year was obviously Adolf Hitler. TIME had a very striking photograph of Adolf in his khaki uniform—not deifying him but making him look very solid and clean and respectable. It began to worry the hell out of me. It was about the time the first atrocity and concentration camp stories were coming in from Germany, and I did not see how TIME could put this dignified picture of Hitler on the cover without implying some sort of tacit endorsement.

I began asking around, but it was December before I stumbled upon a hell of a fine lithograph of a Catherine wheel with naked bodies hanging from it, and down in one corner a tiny little man playing a hymn of hate on an organ, and the man was Hitler. By the time I found it, Harry was off some place and I was alone running the shop. The editors of TIME fell into violent disagreement over my proposal to substitute the lithograph for the colored portrait. In the end, I arbitrated by agreeing with myself and putting the lithograph on.

The day Harry came back I went up to see him. He was standing over a copy of the issue. "Who did this?"

"I did."

"You did?"

Luce's face was white; the blood seemed to have drained even from his lips.

"Have you any idea what you've done? A basic tradition destroyed ... everything I've built ... in one gesture." We simply stood there, eyes fixed on each other.

"Spilt milk," Luce said. "Let's not discuss it."

—*Ralph Ingersoll*

MAN OF 1938
From the unholy organist, a hymn of hate.
(Foreign News)

THEATER

TOSSED OFF?

So well had Playwright Noel Coward planned *Hay Fever* that he wrote it during a house party weekend. *Private Lives* was the product of spending a week's flu-confinement in a Hong Kong hotel. The record is sagging. It took months of voyaging in South American waters to jot down *Design for Living.*   **JAN. 30, 1933**

MUSIC

JIM CROW CONCERT HALL

One of the greatest concert singers of this generation is Marian Anderson, Philadelphia-born Negro contralto. Since she skyrocketed to fame in Salzburg four years ago, the music-lovers and critics of the world's musical capitals have counted it a privilege to hear her sing. Last week it looked as though music-lovers in provincial Washington, D.C., might be denied the privilege. Reason: Washington's only concert hall, Constitution Hall, is owned by the Daughters of the American Revolution, who are so proud they eat mush—much less let a Negro sing from their stage.   **MARCH 6, 1939**

CINEMA

HOOFERS' HOLIDAY

In *The Gay Divorcée* Fred Astaire pursues a young lady (Ginger Rogers) who is seeking divorce from a geologist. There appear the impediments customary in musicomedy romance ... None of it interferes with the elegant genuflections of Astaire, next to Bill Robinson the most nimble-footed hoofer on the U.S. stage.   **OCT. 22, 1934**

MUSIC
FOLK OPERA

For one week *Porgy and Bess*, by Composer George Gershwin, played in Boston, won high praise. On opening night in Manhattan half the Somebodies in town crowded in to hear this latest attempt at a U.S. folk opera ... With music frequently inspired, Mr. Gershwin manages to give new life and importance to the Negroes of Catfish Row. **OCT. 25, 1935**

1934 Embracing reality, "earthy Midwesterner" **Thomas Hart Benton** put America on canvas.

1938 "Marvelous boy" **Orson Welles** bestrode radio and Broadway— and TIME's cover—at 22.

CINEMA
WONDER TOT

Garlanded with laurels at an age when her contemporaries become inflated with conceit about a gold star on the report card, it might seem natural for the most celebrated child alive to be in private life also the most objectionable sample of precocity, weight for age, who ever gave sharp answers to her betters. Such is not the case. Disappointing as the case may be, Shirley Temple is a peewee paragon who obeys her mother, likes raw carrots, eats spinach with enthusiasm, expresses active relish for the taste of cod liver oil. **APRIL 27, 1936**

1939 "Southern decay is no more romantic than decayed teeth" to writer **William Faulkner.**

1939 Carl Sandburg, the biographer and poet, said, "that son-of-a-gun Lincoln grows on you."

LIVING GOD

Into Lhasa, bleak Forbidden City of wind-swept Tibet, last week a swaying caravan brought home Tibet's "living god." This 14th **Dalai Lama,** sovereign pontiff of Tibet, a bright lad of five named Tanchu, had been discovered in China.   **OCT. 9, 1939**

FAREWELL TO THE THRONE

Dignity, like the Imperial mantle which is placed upon England's King at his Coronation, clothed **Edward VIII** and his every act last week after the decision of His Majesty to abdicate. Scarcely anyone failed to tune in on Edward VIII as he said good-by to very nearly all except "the woman I love," **Wallis Simpson.**   **DEC. 21, 1936**

A HARD CASE

Last week the disappearance of **Charles Lindbergh Jr.** from his father's Sourland Mountain home in western New Jersey passed into its third month with the child still missing, the abductors still uncaught ... Scarface Al Capone posted a reward for the child's return.   **MAY 2, 1932**

LOVERS IN A CAR

In Bienville Parish, La. ... one of the Texas deputies sighted a car speeding toward them at 85 m.p.h. It slowed down to pass a truck. The officers shouted an order to halt. Clyde Barrow reached for a gun. The officers fired. The car careened into an embankment. The fusillade continued: 167 shots, 50 of which hit the occupants. Barrow was found with the door of the car half-open and a sawed-off shotgun in his hand. **Bonnie Parker,** wearing a red dress, was doubled up with a machine gun in her lap.

   JUNE 4, 1934

MISSING PERSONS

Set on making a round-the-world flight, the world's No. 1 aviatrix, **Amelia Earhart,** cracked up in Hawaii in her first try three months ago. With her Lockheed Electra patched up, she took off in the opposite direction with ace navigator **Fred Noonan.** July 1 they left Lae, New Guinea for the "worst section"—the 2,550 miles of open ocean where no plane had ever been.   **JULY 12, 1937**

AND HOW THEY GREW

Unlike any other children, **the Dionne Quintuplets** had to have three birthday parties, for they belong to a tremendous public whose agents pay good money to witness their doings.   **MAY 31, 1937**

MOST POPULAR RED

After the Norwegian Government got tired of having him around, **Leon Trotsky** landed in Mexico, began to receive appropriate honors as World Revolutionist No. 1.   **JAN. 25, 1937**

QUEST FOR THE COSMIC RAY

The main purpose of Belgian Professor **Auguste Picard's** stratosphere balloon flight was to record the effect of cosmic rays at high altitudes. At his ceiling of almost eleven miles the rays "were like rain on a tin roof."   **AUG. 29, 1932**

47

PORTRAITS

The Art of the TIME Cover

JOSEPH CONRAD, 1923 Early covers were black and white drawings surrounded by rococo "spinach."

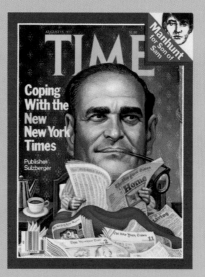

LEOPOLD AMERY, 1927 This cover introduced the red border that has become TIME's enduring symbol.

MARTIN NIEMOLLER, 1940 Ernest Baker's use of background symbols became a template for many covers.

ARTHUR SULZBERGER, 1977 A "flap" highlighting a noncover story appears in the upper-right corner.

TIME FOUNDERS HENRY Luce and Briton Hadden believed powerful individuals could change the course of history—a belief best exemplified in the magazine's annual selection of a Man or Woman of the Year. This fascination with the public deeds (and private lives) of the noted was also reflected each week on the magazine's cover: in TIME's first 50 years, its red border almost always framed a portrait of a newsmaker. Recognizing the historic value and artistic merit of these portraits—many of them the work of noted artists—the National Portrait Gallery of the Smithsonian Institution maintains a permanent collection of some 1,800 paintings and sculptures used on the cover of TIME.

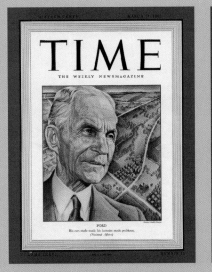

HENRY FORD, 1941 Baker's horizon shows how Ford's flivvers transformed the American landscape.

JOE LOUIS, 1941 Baker painted more than half of TIME's covers that year; this image is one of his finest.

ERNEST HAMLIN BAKER

Between 1939 and 1970, most TIME covers featured highly detailed portraits of newsmakers—and most of them were painted by a trio of artists collectively known to the editors as "the ABCs": Boris Artzybasheff, Ernest Hamlin Baker and Boris Chaliapin.

Ernst Hamlin Baker was the first of the trio to work for TIME; his cover of Poland's Ignace Paderewski appeared in February 1939. It was Baker, working with TIME picture editor Dana Tasker, who developed the look that would be TIME's signature for decades: the subject in the foreground, with symbolic iconography in the background to telegraph the context of his life. The first of these, a painting of German theologian Martin Niemöller (*see facing page*), appeared in 1940. In the 1998 book *Faces of TIME*, Frederick S. Voss describes Baker's technique as "a time-consuming method that began with spending hours scrutinizing photographs of the subject with a magnifying glass and then … making a preliminary drawing, which Baker called a 'facial map,' that delineated the features in minute detail … The result was a crisp image that occasionally seemed brutal in its factuality."*

ALBERT EINSTEIN, 1946 Baker's portrait conflates the physicist's famous equation with its progeny, the dread mushroom cloud of the atom bomb.

DANNY KAYE, 1946 After six years of painting generals, Baker clearly reveled in the star's exuberance.

*This quotation and some biographical material in this section are from FACES OF TIME: 75 YEARS OF TIME MAGAZINE COVER PORTRAITS, by Frederick S. Voss. A Bullfinch Press book in association with the National Portrait Gallery, Smithsonian Institution

ADMIRAL OSAMI NAGANO, 1943 As in Artzybasheff's Yamamoto cover [*page 67*], both man and ship glower.

ADMIRAL KARL DOENITZ, 1943 Sleek with menace, the German U-boat commander eyes the North Atlantic.

BORIS ARTZYBASHEFF

For 24 years—from 1941 to 1965—Boris Artzybasheff graced TIME's cover with a series of portraits that are delightfully whimsical and utterly original. A refugee from the civil wars following the Russian Revolution, Artzybasheff landed in Brooklyn in 1919 with just a few cents (of Turkish money) in his pocket. A gifted draftsman, he was soon flourishing as an illustrator specializing in a sci-fi melding of technology and fantasy.

When Artzybasheff came to TIME—his first cover was of Chinese General Chen Cheng in June 1941—he worked in the standard format developed by Ernest Baker. But Artzybasheff was soon showing his flair for fantasy, which found its best expression in a humorously anthropomorphic blend of the subject and its milieu. Thus, Japanese Admiral Osami Nagano is silhouetted against a Japanese battleship whose guns form a menacing human face, and German U-boat Commander Karl Doenitz becomes a periscope of one of his own vessels. Most memorably, Artzybasheff's witty hands transformed the cranium of visionary (and self-absorbed) architect Buckminster Fuller into his own best-known design, the geodesic dome.

BUCKMINSTER FULLER, 1964 This portrait of the gadfly designer, perhaps Artzybasheff's best-known TIME cover, appeared a year before his death.

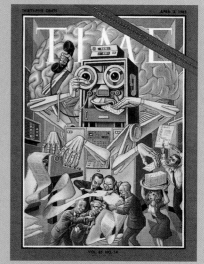

THE COMPUTER IN SOCIETY, 1965 Artzybasheff's humanizing touch found a perfect foil in machinery.

J.P. NEHRU, 1942 Chaliapin turns a verbal cliché—Nehru in Gandhi's shadow—into a haunting image.

BORIS CHALIAPIN

The son of legendary Russian opera singer Feodor Chaliapin, Boris Chaliapin followed his father to Paris in the 1920s to escape the turmoil of the young Soviet Union. Uncomfortable with the prevailing artistic aesthetic in Paris, he then came to America, where his realistic style found a home within TIME's red border. Chaliapin's first cover for the magazine, of Jawaharlal Nehru, appeared in 1942; he was the last of "the ABCs" to join TIME.

Chaliapin had been trained in speed drawing in Paris, and later, in 1942, after he completed a last-minute cover portrait of British General Sir Harold Alexander within 24 hours, he became the artist TIME's editors turned to when faced with a fast change on deadline. He once completed a rush request in only seven hours, whereas Ernest Baker required days, and preferably weeks, for his finely wrought paintings. Yet Chaliapin chafed at being thought of as a speed specialist; that he was a powerful and gifted artist is clear in his 1964 portrait of pianist Thelonious Monk. Chaliapin's bold palette captures with smoldering intensity what it meant to be young, gifted and black in the America of the 1960s.

THELONIOUS MONK, 1964 This searing portrait, scheduled to run in November 1963, was "bumped" by the Kennedy assassination; it ran the following year.

MARSHAL TITO, 1944 Behind him, the ranks of Yugoslav partisans recede into a haze of brushstrokes.

JAMES BYRNES, 1945 The Secretary of State seeks safe harbor in the uncharted seas of a postwar world.

FAMILY VIOLENCE, 1983 The artist posed himself, then scratched, painted and disfigured the result.

SIGMUND FREUD, 1993 Identity crisis? This is not the Viennese guru; it's artist Matt Mahurin in disguise.

MATT MAHURIN

A puzzled Sigmund Freud whose cranium is fragmenting along with his reputation. A father cradling his child—whom he has abused. A primitive man whose face looks startlingly modern. A nuclear terrorist gripping a radioactive pellet. These memorable TIME covers are the work of a master manipulator of images, Matt Mahurin—and, incredibly, each of these covers is actually a portrait of the artist. A gifted photographer, Mahurin often uses self-portraits as the first step in the creation of an image; he estimates he has appeared on TIME's cover 10 or 12 times over the years, though always in disguise.

For his first TIME cover—a 1983 story on family violence—Mahurin, then only 23, posed with a doll, then painted and altered successive iterations of the picture to achieve a sinister effect. For the cover on Freud's reputation, Mahurin dyed his goatee white and dressed up as the psychoanalyst, complete with bald cap, then altered the image on his computer to achieve the puzzle effect. (Says Mahurin: "The folks in the TIME art department didn't recognize me—they kept saying, 'Matt, what's going on? No color pictures of Freud exist!' ") *Homo erectus* also began as a self-portrait, and the heavy ridge over the eyebrows is a truly "digital" effect— Mahurin blended close-ups of his knuckles onto his face to achieve it.

HOMO ERECTUS, 1994 Mahurin changed his blue eyes to brown to match current scientific models of early man. He drew the ear and neck by hand.

NUCLEAR TERRORIST, 1994 To get this effect, Mahurin put a shower cap on his face—and took a deep breath.

FASHION MAGS: DIRTY LAUNDRY

JUNE 5, 1995

$2.95

Master Of the Universe

Having conquered the world's computers, BILL GATES takes aim at banks, phone companies, even Hollywood. He's in for the fight of his life.

BILL GATES, 1994 Eschewing computer tricks, Heisler seeks "an undeniable realism ... These images make you say, 'Hey, what's going on here?'"

KHRUSHCHEV'S SECRET TAPES

S&L HONCHOS FEEL THE HEAT

David Lynch
The Wild-at-Art Genius Behind *Twin Peaks*

Hollywood's Big-Budget Blockbusters

Bush's Bad Cop

From taxes to clean air, JOHN SUNUNU is the power to reckon with

DAVID LYNCH, 1990 Double exposure: with a lighting change and a blink, Lynch is looking two ways at once.

JOHN SUNUNU, 1990 In Heisler's lens, George Bush's tough chief of staff melts into an American flag.

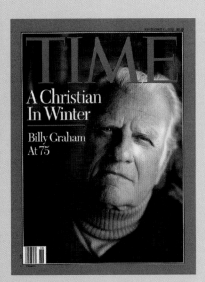

A Christian In Winter

Billy Graham At 75

BILLY GRAHAM, 1993 Beyond his flair for special effects, Gregory Heisler is a master of the art of portraiture.

GREGORY HEISLER

Bill Gates, the wizard of software, appears on TIME's cover as a Promethean figure who holds glowing energy within his hand. A computer-enhanced photograph? Not at all: this picture is the work of a different wizard, Gregory Heisler, whose unique camera skills have made him the photographer TIME calls upon for special portraits, including seven of the eight Man of the Year covers in the 1990s. In Heisler's photograph of Gates, the computer tycoon is simply holding a strip of polyester plastic: at just the right camera angle, the "lightning bolt" leaps into life.

Heisler's signature is the creation of special effects—not through darkroom tricks or digital enhancement, but within the camera. A famous example: his photo of TIME's Men of the Year for 1991, "The Two George Bushes" [*see page 157*]. Rather than combine separate pictures on a computer, Heisler first clicked his shutter as the President looked to his left, then captured him on the same sheet of film looking the opposite way. Before his 15-minute session with Bush, Heisler spent 25 hours in the studio using a stand-in for the President to position his camera for the shot. Result: magic.

DWIGHT EISENHOWER, 1959 Celebrated Realist Andrew Wyeth, himself a two-time cover subject, painted Ike.

V.I. LENIN, 1964 Ben Shahn, a veteran of the social upheavals of the 1930s, was the right man to paint Lenin.

PRINCE CHARLES, 1969 At the end of the psychedelic '60s, Peter Max portrayed Britain's Prince as a pop star.

JOHN UPDIKE, 1982 A perfect pairing of two masters of close scrutiny: novelist Updike by portraitist Alex Katz.

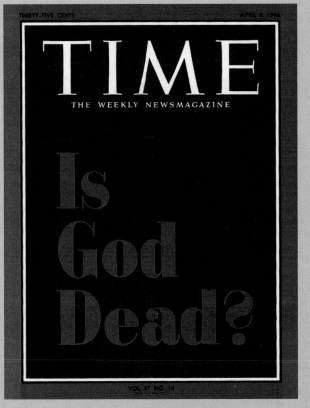

IS GOD DEAD? 1966 With the subject unavailable to pose, an all-type query became TIME's most memorable cover.

ROBERT KENNEDY, 1968 Just weeks before R.F.K.'s murder, Pop artist Roy Lichtenstein caught his celebrity appeal.

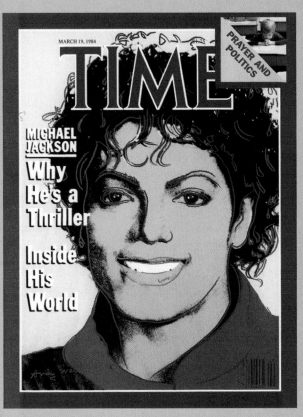

MICHAEL JACKSON, 1984 Who better to capture a singular sensation at the peak of his fame than Andy Warhol?

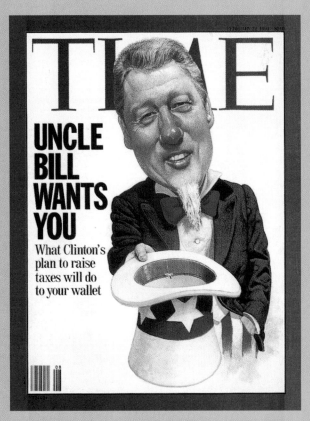

BILL CLINTON, 1993 In satirist C.F. Payne's hands, Clinton was Uncle Sam—and Newt Gingrich was Uncle Scrooge.

WAR

The evils of Nazism
and the shock of
Pearl Harbor drew
the nation into a
conflict that would
establish America
as a world power

FIGHTING THE BLAZEBLITZ

London has seen it this bad only once since the Great Fire of 1666—a month ago, when the first great incendiary raid burned out blocks of the City, made night day and framed the dome of historic St. Paul's in a thick drapery of acrid smoke. Since then London has learned how to deal with the *blazeblitz*. The secret is to douse each bomb within a minute or two. When the incendiaries fall, crackling into blue- and rose-colored flares, crowds of householders in all stages of undress pop from doorways and pounce on the bombs. **JAN. 27, 1941**

Bruce W. Nelan

THE LAST GOOD WAR

World War II set a standard that has been difficult to match

MANY AMERICANS WHO LIVED THROUGH WHAT WAS THE MOST DESTRUCTIVE war in history still refer to it as "the last good war." Not that any war is good and not that there weren't terrible sacrifices, but World War II, as TIME dubbed it, was a war that had to be fought and won. This was an unambiguous struggle between good and evil. It was not just about national interests but also about values. Hitler and Tojo had to be defeated; there was no doubt about it.

The U.S. was the "home front"; the "war effort" was priority No. 1; and complaints were met with a standard reply: "Don't you know there's a war on?" The country felt very close to its far-off troops—sons, nephews, the kids who lived down the street. They were "our boys." The unity of belief, purpose and effort felt surprisingly good.

At the center of the war's vast changes was the military—transformed by the nation into a colossus and, in turn, transforming the nation into a superpower. From an Army of 1.7 million and a Navy of 160,000 on the eve of Pearl Harbor, America's armed forces grew to number 12.3 million men and women by May 1945.

The parades and the generous G.I. Bill of Rights that welcomed these veterans home were a new experience for a country that had never gone willingly into foreign entanglements. Only late in World War I was Woodrow Wilson finally forced to send a New World expeditionary force to rescue the Old. Even then American opinion was not fully convinced it was necessary to fight Kaiser Bill. When the victorious doughboys sailed home, they were almost ignored, and when they marched into Washington to demand a promised veterans' bonus, the U.S. Army—led by future World War II hero Douglas A. MacArthur—drove them out of town.

No war since 1945 has been as popular. Korea was a strung-out, bitter bloodletting that ended in a stalemate. What ever happened to unconditional surrender? That had been the victory slogan for World War II, and the U.S. now seemed to expect nothing less every time.

If Korea was not a good war, Vietnam was a distinctly bad one. The 15-year struggle in Indochina was even bloodier, more costly and harder to understand than Korea, and its support ebbed away. As the war wore on, it filled U.S. streets with demonstrators, tore up university campuses, split society and families, dragged down a President and came close to destroying the Army. While the G.I.s of World War II were loved, the grunts of Vietnam, no longer "our boys" in the same way, were reviled and sometimes spit on.

GRENADA AND PANAMA, MERE INCIDENTS, WERE OVER TOO SOON to be judged. The U.S. military's redemption had to wait until the Gulf War in 1991—at last, another good war. National interests—oil and gas—were at stake, and so were values. Again, the enemy was a mustache-wearing dictator who had invaded his neighbor. A fair number of Americas were hesitant, but the morale-boosting triumph came quickly, with few casualties among the troops—all of whom were tough, highly trained professionals.

So the war against Iraq joined World War II as a standard for a good war, one that the American people could support fully and feel was just. It is a very challenging standard indeed, for it requires the fortuitous combination of an evil enemy, a vital national stake in the struggle, an overwhelming victory and—now—low casualties. In the future, very few conflicts will meet it. ■

POLAND

MURDER IN THE FIELDS

[*An account by free-lance photographer Julien Bryan accompanied this picture.*] A few minutes before, several German planes had bombed a farmhouse. They went away, and after a while seven Polish women who were desperately in need of food went out to scratch for potatoes. But the planes hadn't really gone away. They doubled back and, flying along as low as 200 feet, opened up their machine guns. The women tried to run away. But two were killed. I was talking with the survivors when a little girl—ten or eleven—ran up. Her sister was one of the dead. We helped her find the body. **OCT. 16, 1939**

OCCUPIED EUROPE

GHOSTS OF THE GHETTOS

The American Jewish Congress reported that by late 1942, 2,000,000 Jews had been massacred. *Vernichtungskolonnen* (extermination squads) rounded them up and killed them with machine guns, lethal gas, high-voltage electricity and hunger. Almost all were stripped before they died; their clothes were needed by the Nazis. The Warsaw ghetto is empty. The streets crowded only a year ago are silent now. **MARCH 8, 1943**

1942 Master strategist **Admiral Erich Raeder** of Hitler's Navy: "a short-legged pouter pigeon."

1944 Britain's **General Bernard Montgomery** was "wry, spry, sharp-faced … picturesque."

1944 "Kindly, soft-spoken" U.S. **Gen. Omar Bradley** boasted a "keen, analytical mind."

1945 Gen. George S. Patton: "the swift, slashing halfback for Coach Eisenhower."

FRANCE

ARMISTICE AND AFTER

Roles changed quickly in Europe last week. Patriots became traitors and exiles, and conquerors became sightseers. Foremost sightseer was a little man in a light brown duster … Adolf Hitler gazed down at the tomb of Napoleon Bonaparte, whose star had soared to a zenith equalled only by his own before it sputtered and plunged. Accompanied by a staff of art historians and architectural experts, the Führer visited the Opéra, strolled through the galleries of the half-emptied Louvre, went to the top of the Eiffel Tower where a swastika waved. **JULY 8, 1940**

BRITAIN

THE LANDMARKS FALL

History received its most mortal wounds in London last week. The Mother of Parliaments, Westminster Abbey, the British Museum were all hit in one night of explosion even more desecrating than the City bombing of last December. The House of Commons Chamber, where Disraeli argued with Gladstone in the days when the Empire was being completed, where Prime Minister Herbert Asquith told the members of Parliament that World War I had begun, was gutted by seven high-explosive bombs just 72 hours after Winston Churchill had there spun one of his finest fabrics of oratory. **MAY 19, 1941**

JUNE NIGHT

Twenty-four hours were left to bid the battle teams a last Godspeed. In the morning "Ike" Eisenhower stood at an English quayside, chinning in his friendly Kansas way with embarking Tommies. In the afternoon he called newsmen into his trailer tent, told them of the great decision. He slouched in his chair, grinned lopsidedly, chain-smoked cigarets, wisecracked a bit, once leaped like an uncoiled spring to exclaim: "The sun is out!" All evening his khaki staff car, marked with the four red stars, rolled across the sleeping landscape … Night cloaked the countryside and the airdromes were humming with preparation when he gave his last "good luck." **JUNE 12, 1944**

UNDER FIRE: A U.S. soldier hits the Normandy beach in Robert Capa's famous photograph

BERLIN

DEATH RATTLE

The world's fourth city, in its dying hours, was a monstrous thing of almost utter destruction. Where shells had not amputated the trunks of century-old lindens, there were soft, green leaves, and they fluttered down and stuck like bright greeting cards on the Russian tanks' hot grey armor. … *Katusha* rockets screeched over the Brandenburger Tor. Then, against a background of flames, the Red banner of victory was unfurled over the gutted Reichstag.   **MAY 7, 1945**

ITALY

THE END OF IL DUCE

[*A first-person account by* TIME *correspondent Reg Ingraham.*] This Sunday morning in a sun-drenched square not far from Milan's center, where 22 years ago Editor Benito Mussolini launched the Black Shirt March on Rome, his battered, bullet-riddled corpse sprawled in public display. His head rested on the breast of his mistress, comely Clara Petacci, who had died with him. A howling mob was struggling for place beside the heap of cadavers. The bodies lay on the ground for many hours. Then, to give the mob a better view, the partisans hanged them by their feet from a scaffold on the Piazza.   **MAY 7, 1945**

BUCHENWALD

BACK FROM THE GRAVE

[*A first-person account by* TIME *correspondent Percy Knauth.*] In the terrible barracks of the Small Camp, the starving men lay packed like rotting cargo on bare wooden shelves reaching from the floor to the ceiling … it was all I could do to stand the sight and smell of the parodies of human beings who inhabited them. They were alive by instinct only, and by instinct they almost knocked me down when I produced from my pocket one pitiful chocolate bar in answer to a plea of a prisoner for food. At the sight of that morsel of food these filthy, spidery human beings were galvanized by a single impulse: to get a crumb, just a crumb of something to put into their stomachs.   **MAY 14, 1945**

MAN OF THE YEAR 1939–1947

1940 Adolf Hitler conquered five nations by arms in 1940, but Britain stood firm, and Prime Minister **Winston Churchill** was named Man of the Year. Warned TIME: "Before the end of 1941, Adolf Hitler may be Man of the Century—if Britain falls."

1939 Signing a secret pact with an old enemy, **Joseph Stalin** paved the way for Hitler's war.

1941 After preparing a reluctant U.S. for battle, **Franklin D. Roosevelt** faced two potent foes.

1942 Hitler betrayed **Joseph Stalin** and invaded Russia—and the U.S. gained a new ally.

1943 Overseeing a vast war effort on two fronts, **Gen. George Marshall** built a professional army.

1944 Leading the Allies into France, **Gen. Dwight D. Eisenhower** rolled back the Germans.

1947 A general turned diplomat, **George Marshall** followed James Byrnes as Truman's Secretary of State. He battled the expansionist Soviets with the Truman Doctrine and oversaw the visionary Marshall Plan that rebuilt a bankrupt Europe.

1945 Initially scorned as unable to fill F.D.R.'s shoes, **Harry S. Truman** soon proved his mettle.

1946 **James Byrnes** was the first Secretary of State to face a perilous new era: the Cold War.

PEARL HARBOR

SURPRISE ATTACK!

It was Sunday midday, clear and sunny. Many a citizen was idly listening to the radio when the flash came that the Japanese had attacked Hawaii. In Topeka they were listening to *The Spirit of '41* and napping on their sofas after dinner. In San Francisco, where it was not quite noon, they were listening to the news, Philharmonic and *Strings in Swingtime*. In Portland, Maine, where it was cold but still sunny, they were lining up for the movies.

For the first time in its history, the U.S. at war was attacked first. Out on the Pacific and in the islands the great drama of U.S. history was coming to a climax. Over the U.S. and its history there was a great unanswered question: What would the people, the 132,000,000, say in the face of the mightiest event of their time?

What they said—tens of thousands of them—was: "Why, the yellow bastards!"

DEC. 15, 1941

SAVED: A small craft rescues a sailor who fled the smoking U.S.S. *West Virginia*. In the rear, also hit, is the U.S.S. *Tennessee*

1941 Admiral Isoroku Yamamoto's surprise attack was "wily as only the Japanese can be."

1942 U.S. **Admiral William Halsey** had "a face like a battlefield … big, broad, strong."

1944 Japan's **Admiral Shigetaro Shimada**— "dull, pursed-lipped, little"—headed the Navy.

1944 "Tart, taciturn" **Gen. Joseph Stilwell** was a "red-tape-be-damned anti-diplomat."

THE PHILIPPINES

PROMISE KEPT

Last week, on the flag bridge of the 10,000-ton, 614-ft. light cruiser *Nashville*, stood a proud, erect figure in freshly pressed khaki. Douglas MacArthur had come back to the Philippines, as he had promised. He had slept well, eaten a hearty breakfast. Now with his corncob pipe he pointed over the glassy, green waters of Leyte (rhymes with 8-A) Gulf, where rode the greatest fleet ever assembled in the Southwest Pacific. On the horizon loomed the majestic battleships of Admiral William F. Halsey's Third Fleet—some of them ghosts from the graveyard of Pearl Harbor. There was not a Japanese craft in sight.

OCT. 30, 1944

THE PHILIPPINES

MARCH OF DEATH

[*Full reports of the treatment of captured U.S. soldiers on Bataan in 1942 did not reach the U.S. until three years later.*] On the "March of Death" gaunt, unshaven soldiers tramped day after day without hats under the tropical sun. Hundreds were flogged, starved and beheaded. Sometimes their hands were trussed behind their backs and sometimes they got short rests while strutting Jap guards stood by, ready with rifle butt or bayonet for the slightest break from abject docility. Prisoners got almost no food, were often stripped of their canteens. Prisoners who fell out were killed, or buried alive. Many were left where they lay, for the animals and birds. **MARCH 12, 1945**

IWO JIMA

LIVES FOR YARDS

[*An eyewitness account by* TIME *reporter Robert Sherrod.*] It was sickening to watch the Jap mortar shells crash into the men as they climbed. These huge explosive charges—"floating ash cans" we called them—would crash among the thin lines of marines or among the boats bringing reinforcements to the beach, throwing sand, water and even pieces of human flesh 100 feet into the air. By noon the assault battalions reported 20 to 25% fatalities.   **MARCH 5, 1945**

SURRENDER

VICTORY'S GRIM VISAGE

[*An eyewitness account by* TIME *reporter Theodore H. White.*] Complete silence greeted the Japanese as they ascended the deck. The American generals watched them with varying degrees of emotion. Stilwell bristled like a dog at the sight of an enemy. Spaatz' chiseled face lines were sharp in contempt. Kenney curled his lips in a visible sneer.   **SEPT. 10, 1945**

HIROSHIMA

THE BOMB

The greatest and most terrible of wars ended, this week, in the echoes of an enormous event—an event so much more enormous that, relative to it, the war itself shrank to minor significance. The knowledge of victory was as charged with sorrow and doubts, as with joy and gratitude.

With the controlled splitting of the atom, humanity, already profoundly perplexed and disunified, was brought inescapably into a new age in which all thoughts and things were split— and far from controlled. The rational mind had won the most Promethean of its conquests over nature, and had put into the hands of common man the fire and force of the sun itself. Was man equal to the challenge?

AUG. 20, 1945

FAREWELL TO THE HOUSE HE BUILT

In The Bronx, **Babe Ruth** put on his old uniform for the last time: in a home-plate ceremony at Yankee Stadium the uniform and the Bambino's celebrated old number 3 were officially retired. **JUNE 21, 1948**

SYMPHONIC SINATRA

The announcement of **Frank Sinatra's** appearance at the Hollywood Bowl had thrown Los Angeles high-brow music lovers into a self-righteous williwaw, the King of Swoon's fans at Pasadena into a squealing ecstasy. **AUG. 23, 1947**

"HELLO, BOYS"

Marlene Dietrich, back after eleven months of U.S.O.ing in Europe, greeted returning soldiers by standing at the end of a Manhattan pier and waving a leg at them. She drew a deafening roar and a blizzard of coins. Then she had herself boosted to a porthole and really got down to cases. In Europe, she said, her most effective line was just: "Hello, boys." **JULY 30, 1945**

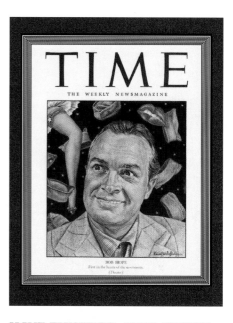

HAVE TUXEDOS; WILL TRAVEL

When it looked as if his U.S.O. tour of Alaska would fall through, **Bob Hope** wired: "WE SING, DANCE, TELL STORIES; HAVE TUXEDOES; WILL TRAVEL; CAN WE PLAY YOUR CIRCUIT?" **SEPT. 20, 1943**

OPTIMISTIC ZIGGURAT

A spry old man, as regal-looking as a Shakespearean actor, **Frank Lloyd Wright** unwrapped his model for "The Modern Gallery of Non-Objective Painting." To some newsmen, the model looked like a big, white ice cream freezer. **OCT. 1, 1945**

LITTLE FLOWER ON THE AIR

Every Sunday since 1941, on his radio show *Talk to the People*, unpredictable New York City Mayor **Fiorello LaGuardia** has growled at chiselers, sang sarcastically at enemies, squeaked angrily at hecklers. **DEC. 10, 1945**

ROOKIE OF THE YEAR

Jackie Robinson stops and starts as though turned off & on with a toggle switch. He seems to hit a baseball on the dead run. Once in motion, he wobbles along, elbows flying, hips swaying, shoulders rocking ... He is not only jack-rabbit fast, but about one thought and two steps ahead of every base-runner in the business. **SEPT. 22, 1947**

·OLICEMAN'S LOT

. **Edgar Hoover** is seldom seen without a male companion, most frequently solemn-faced Clyde ·olson, his assistant. His reason: ·is dread that someone ... will ·lant a naked woman in his path, ·y to frame him. **MAR. 11, 1940**

OF TRUTH AND SHAME

Said Jawaharlal Nehru: "I have a sense of utter shame." Shame spread through the world with the news of **Mahatma Gandhi's** murder. The event brought the shock of recognition, rather than the shock of surprise. More forcibly than anyone in his age, he had asserted that love was the law; how else should he die but through hatred? He had warned against the glib, the new, the plausible; how else should he die, but by a pistol in the hands of a young intellectual? **FEB. 9, 1948**

AFFLUENCE

THE BOOM ...
Affluence and the
automobile drove
families out of the cities
into cookie-cutter
suburbs like Long
Island's Levittown

America soared as the world's economic superpower, even as it contended with the specter of expanding Communist empires

Underneath America's prosperous veneer lurked the threat of nuclear annihilation. Here, a Detroit family tests its fallout shelter

Howard Chua-Eoan

SOMEWHERE OVER THE DASHBOARD

History through America's once and future dream machines

ET'S BEGIN WITH THE TALE OF THE FIN, ITS RISE AND FALL from the American car and the American Dream. The design staff at General Motors copied the first fins off a top-secret U.S. Air Force plane (the Lockheed P-38), quietly grafting them as little bumps on the rear of the 1948 Cadillac. The next year's model was a best seller, and as the 1950s progressed, the fins proliferated. They appeared on Oldsmobiles, on Buicks, on Chryslers, with Fords finally sprouting them in 1957. The fins, fickle as Paris hemlines, grew wide and high, rising to 40 in. off the ground on the '59 Cadillac Eldorado.

These cathedral spires of the highway were gaudy advertisements for an America that owned three-quarters of the earth's cars. Automobiles were the symbols as well as the vehicles of individual and national progress, so why shouldn't Americans have the most ostentatious models—with new fins each year? At the height of fin fashion, American cars (with sticker prices about the cost of a Levittown house) resembled the pagoda-shouldered pottery courtesans in Tang dynasty tombs—exotica from a lost age of extravagance. The 1958 recession began the style's decline. Fin *de siècle*.

The symbiosis of car and economy, which continues to this day, gave rise to the motel (the first chain, Holiday Inn, started in 1952) and to the Golden Arches (Ray Kroc bought the fledgling roadside food chain of the McDonald brothers in 1961). Las Vegas grew out of traffic, with Californians driving in on Highway 91 at the rate of 20,000 a weekend (they're still coming).

Between 1945 and 1955, the number of cars in the U.S. doubled from 26 million to 52 million. That boom, along with the highways that supported it, extended the

strange and strained realm of suburbia. To absorb this burgeoning mobility came drive-in theaters, drive-in restaurants, drive-in banks, and, most important of all, the shopping mall—Main Street reconfigured for cars. Society was transfigured: the automobile drove America to a new frontier made up of Tinkertoy communities full of undefined relationships and spaces, with the car itself an extension of living room, playroom, bedroom, with the whole country viewed through the windshield.

"MAMA, CARS DON'T BEHAVE. THEY ARE BEHAVED UPON," THE SON IN *DRIVING MISS DAISY* TELLS his mother when she tries to blame her Packard for an accident. But cars are more active par-

ticipants than that: they bear witness to so much human fame and folly. They reflect opulence (Jayne Mansfield's mink-trimmed Mark II) and understatement (the Volkswagen Beetle's populari-ty). Cars create heroes (Lee Iacocca, who conceived of the Ford Mustang and later saved Chrysler) and failures (John DeLorean, whose sleek, eponymous brainstorm was an egotistical disaster).

And they are the chariots of mythology: from the silver Porsche 550 Spyder that James Dean drove to his death in 1955 to the dark blue 1961 Lincoln Continental phaeton that ferried John F. Kennedy to his assassina-tion to the white Ford Bronco that O.J. Simpson rode to infamy. Cars are America's time machines, moving us forward even as they connect us to the past. The movie *Back to the Future* figured that out in 1985: its time travelers zip back and forth in a souped-up DeLorean. There may be hope for fins yet. ∎

THE PRESIDENCY

SURPRISE!

The press (TIME and LIFE included) had planned post-election issues on the seemingly safe basis that Dewey was in. Even when they were confronted by the actual news that proved them wrong, some editors refused to believe it, or report it. The morning after the election, the face of the U.S. press wore a ludicrous look. **NOV. 15, 1948**

KOREA

THE UGLY WAR

[*A firsthand report by* TIME & LIFE *correspondent John Osborne.*] This is a story that no American should ever have to write. It is the ugly story of an ugly war ... The American effort and the American soldier in Korea are magnificent ... [but] our leaders must grasp one quite simple fact: war against the Communists of Asia cannot be won—not really won—by military means alone. To attempt to win it so is to force upon our men in the field acts and attitudes of the utmost savagery. This means not the usual, inevitable savagery of combat in the field, but savagery in detail—the blotting out of villages where the enemy *may* be hiding; the shooting and shelling of refugees who *may* include North Koreans in the anonymous white clothing of the Korean countryside, or who *may* be screening an enemy marching upon our position. **AUG. 21, 1950**

BERLIN

PURCHASE OF FREEDOM

Last Sunday, the first sunny day in weeks, Berliners forgot about their usual meager pleasures and instead went out to Tempelhof Airport. Sitting amid the ruins surrounding the infield, perched on trees and fences, they watched the steady, reassuring stream of planes roaring out of the skies ... In the thronged square of of Melsungen, an old walled town in Hesse only 22 miles from the Soviet zone's border, Social Democratic Leader Ernst Spars climbed onto a platform. He pointed to the overcast skies which had for two weeks been filled with the roar of U.S. planes carrying food to besieged Berlin. "Up there," cried Spars, "the American people are showing their faith in the cause of our Berlin brothers every hour of every day." **JULY 19, 1948**

THE SOUTH

CRISIS IN ARKANSAS

Most of the Negro children came in a group, accompanied by adults, and left quietly when told by a National Guardsman that "Governor Faubus has placed this school off limits to Negroes." But little Elizabeth Eckford, 15, stepped alone from a bus ... In a neat cotton dress, bobby-sox and ballet slippers, she walked straight to the National Guard line on the sidewalk. The Guardsmen raised their rifles, keeping her out. "Go home, you burr head," rasped an adult voice. Elizabeth, clutching tight at her notebook, began a long, slow walk down the two blocks fronting the school.   **SEPT. 16, 1957**

THE SOUTH

WHAT THEY WERE UP TO

Overnight the word flashed throughout the various Negro neighborhoods: support Rosa Parks; don't ride the buses Monday. Within 48 hours mimeographed leaflets were out, calling for a one-day bus boycott. A white woman saw one of the leaflets and called the Montgomery *Advertiser,* demanding that it print the story "to show what the niggers are up to." The *Advertiser* did—and publicized the boycott plan among Negroes in a way that they themselves could never have achieved ... On Monday Montgomery Negroes walked, rode mules, drove horse-drawn buggies, traveled to work in private cars.   **FEB. 18, 1957**

1948 "Los Alamos and its aftermath left **J. Robert Oppenheimer** with a legacy of concern."

1954 "The first full-dress **H-blast** turned a mid-Pacific sandspit into a submarine crater."

1954 Intense **Adm. Hyman Rickover:** "His passage leaves a boiling wake of lacerated egos."

1957 "Rumpled, shaggy-browed" physicist **Edward Teller:** "the father of the H-bomb."

INVESTIGATIONS

THE GAUGE OF RECKLESSNESS

What will probably be remembered as the most memorable scene of the McCarthy-Army hearings occurred on the 30th day. Army Counsel Joseph Welch was winding up his dogged cross-examination of Roy Cohn when Joe McCarthy commandeered the microphone … Without any warning or relevancy, McCarthy interjected the name of Fred Fisher, 32, an associate in Welch's Boston law firm. Fisher, said McCarthy, "has been for a number of years" a member of the National Lawyers Guild, "the legal bulwark of the Communist Party." When McCarthy had finished his harangue, Welch slowly and with great sadness spoke up: "Until this moment, Senator, I think I never really gauged your cruelty and your recklessness … Let us assassinate this lad no further. You have done enough. Have you no sense of decency, sir? At long last have you left no sense of decency?" There was a moment of profound silence, then a roll of thunderous applause.   **JUNE 21, 1954**

MOSCOW

THE KITCHEN DEBATE

Looking over the ranch house's sleek, gadget-stocked kitchen, Khrushchev showed, as he did dozens of times at the U.S. exhibition in Moscow, the braggy defensiveness that seems to come over Soviet officials when they confront the U.S. standard of living.

Khrushchev: You Americans think that the Russian people will be astonished to see these things. The fact is that all our new houses have this kind of equipment.

Nixon: We don't claim to astonish your people. We hope to show our diversity and our right to choose. We do not want one government official [saying] all houses should be the same. **AUG. 3, 1959**

PALESTINE

TRADING IN TERROR

In Palestine, in the hills overlooking the Garden of Gethsemane, Arabs and Jews bombarded each other with mortar and grenades. In an orange grove near Rehovoth, Jews bombed a British train bringing soldiers back from leave in Cairo. In the twisted steel and splintered wood, 28 were found dead or wounded. The terrorist Stern Gang of extremist Zionists boasted that it had blown up the train [in retaliation for] the preceding week's horror in Jerusalem's Ben Yehuda street, where an explosion had killed 54 Jews. Arabs took the credit for setting off the blast, but the Jews preferred to believe it had been the work of British agents. **MARCH 8, 1948**

CUBA

CAREER REBEL

Today in Cuba no name moves men more quickly to praise—or to anger—than that of Fidel Castro. To the people of Oriente he is a romantic near legend. To President Fulgencio Batista he is a nagging threat to the strongman's position as boss of Cuba. Last December Castro landed a force of 82 seasick men in Oriente, set up headquarters in the wilderness of the Sierra Maestra. Castro knows that he cannot win merely by avoiding capture. But he does want to become a symbol of opposition. **JULY 8, 1957**

CHINA

MEETING THE CONQUEROR

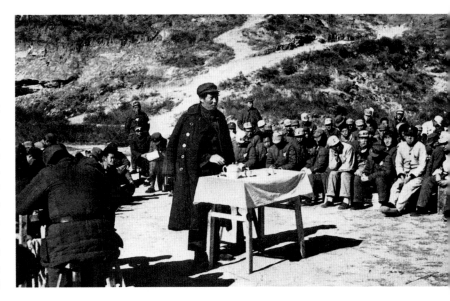

Barring miracles, Chiang Kai-shek was beaten. Most (if not all) of China would soon be added to the eleven countries or parts of countries run by the Communists. Control of all China, together with the areas he already held, would place 40% of the world's population in Stalin's grasp. Chiang still held (nominally) far more territory than he had in the worst years of the Japanese war. Then, however, most Chinese wanted him to keep on resisting the enemy. Now, it seemed, most Chinese wanted him to quit. For the third time in 21 years Peiping's citizens prepared to receive an approaching conqueror. **DEC. 27, 1948**

HUNGARY

PORTRAIT OF DEATH

Out of Budapest last week LIFE brought unforgettable pictures that added up to the most eloquent report of Hungary's bloody fight against tyranny, the work of a free-lance photographer named John Sadovy. His grim shots of fury, terror and the face of death were all the more remarkable for the cold courage he needed to take them in a confused, vengeful rebellion in which the bullets zinged from all directions. His most memorable sequence: rebels cutting down security police as they poured out of a Communist headquarters. **NOV. 19, 1956**

SHOW BUSINESS

WALT'S TOY

Once upon a time, in the magic realm of California, there was a grown-up heady boy named Walt Disney who set out to create the happiest place on earth. So he went into his countinghouses and to his moneylenders, and he collected millions of dollars. Then he ordered his royal artists and carpenters to build a whimsical wonderland of spaceships to the moon and Mark Twain river boats, of mechanical monkeys and bobbing hippos, of moated castles, wilderness forts and make-believe jungles. All the children, young and old, came to visit this happy place, called Disneyland. And Walt made millions happily ever after.

Last week, Disneyland celebrated its second birthday, and Walt Disney was indeed the world's biggest boy with the world's biggest toy. Even adults can lose themselves in Disneyland, where the past they have not seen melts into the future they will never know.   **JULY 29, 1957**

SPACE

A TIME OF DANGER

Somewhere out of the desolate steppes of the Soviet Union a giant rocket roared off into space last week, putting the second Soviet satellite, which carried an experimental dog named Little Curly, into orbit more than 1,000 miles above earth. Sputnik II weighed 1,120.8 lbs., six times the weight of Sputnik I, heavier than many types of nuclear warheads. The Soviet rocket generated a total thrust more than enough to power an atomic bomb to the moon, more than enough to power a missile around the earth.   **NOV. 11, 1957**

MAN OF THE YEAR 1948–1960

1948 Harry S Truman "gave 'em hell"—and scored a stunning upset of opponent Tom Dewey.

1949 In a class of his own: **Winston Churchill** was named TIME's Man of the Half-Century.

1950 As the cold war heated up in Korea, the U.S. soldier—**G.I. Joe**—marched into history.

1951 Mohammed Mossadegh rallied a short-lived anti-Western government in Iran.

1952 The coronation of young, energetic **Queen Elizabeth II** ushered in a new era for Britain.

1953 West Germany's **Konrad Adenauer** forced his war-shattered nation to face the future.

1954 Secretary of State **John Foster Dulles** brought "brinkmanship" to the cold war lexicon.

1955 Detroit's **Harlow H. Curtice** helped steer the U.S. into a new age of wide-open affluence.

1956 The **Hungarian Patriot** launched the first revolt behind the Soviets' "Iron Curtain."

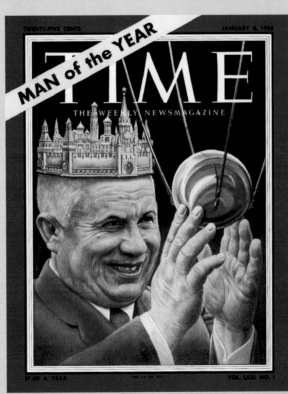

1957 With the unexpected launch of the world's first satellite, Sputnik, Soviet leader **Nikita Khrushchev** scored an immense propaganda victory over the U.S. and transformed the cold war into an ongoing duel for scientific supremacy: the Space Race.

1958 A crisis in Algeria brought World War II hero **Charles de Gaulle** back to power in France.

1959 Facing up to the high-flying Khrushchev, **Dwight D. Eisenhower** rallied the NATO allies.

1960 U.S. Scientists scored impressive gains as they struggled to keep pace with the Soviets.

MUSIC

HI LUH-HUH-HUH-HUV-YEW

In a pivoting stance, his hips swing sensuously from side to side and **Elvis Presley's** entire body takes on a frantic quiver, as if he had swallowed a jackhammer. His throat seems full of desperate aspirates ("Hi want you, hi need you, hi luh-huh-huh-huv yew-hew") or hiccuping glottis strokes, and his diction is poor. **MAY 14, 1956**

THEATER

RUMBLE ON BROADWAY

West Side Story suggests that the salvation of the serious Broadway musical may lie in neither text nor music—which, trying to coalesce, all too often merely collide—but in dancing. Choreographer Jerome Robbins has made the feet that propel the production equally the shoulders on which it rests. His switch-blade rumblers jeer and snort, crouch and slither and spring ... After the opening, at a full-blast party, rooters swarmed over Robbins, while the dark-haired girls and long-haired boys of the cast sipped champagne, danced to music from *My Fair Lady*. **OCT. 7, 1957**

MUSIC
BERETS AND BEBOP

Bebop is a way of life (slogan: "be hip, be sharp, be bop!"). Its feverish practitioners like to wear berets, goatees and green-tinted horn-rimmed glasses, talk about their "interesting new sounds." Bebop is screechingly loud. It is also breathlessly fast, with some biting dissonance and shifty rhythms. Its high priest is **Dizzy Gillespie,** 30, a South Carolina boy whose rapid-fire, scattershot talk has about the same pace—and content—as his music.   **MAY 17, 1949**

1949 Milton Berle: "a brash, strongbow-shaped mouth ... expert timing, tireless bounce."

CINEMA
BOY MEETS GHOUL

Barely a celebrity when he was killed in a sports-car crack-up eleven months ago, actor **James Dean** last week was a teen-age craze, haunting U.S. news-stands, which are plastered with four fast-selling magazines devoted wholly to him. Marveled one West Coast cynic: "This is something new in Hollywood—boy meets ghoul."   **SEPT. 3, 1956**

1952 Lucille Ball brought to TV a "cheerful rowdiness rare since the days of silent movies."

1955 Ed Sullivan: "On camera ... a stone-faced monument just off the boat from Easter Island."

ART
THE WILD ONES

Advance-guard painting is wild, woolly, willful. Its pro-consuls, **Jackson Pollock** and Willem de Kooning ... concentrated all the forces they could muster on the smallest possible problem: to express what they happened to be feeling in the process of painting. The results were huge canvases excitedly smeared, spattered, daubed, dribbled and gobbed with color in the shape of free-wheeling overall designs, as if the artists had been playing with paints and got carried away.   **FEB. 20, 1956**

1958 Jack Paar, dean of late night: "one of a new class of TV-age enter-tainers—the just-talkers."

AN ICON IS BORN

Marilyn Monroe is a saucy, hip-swinging 5-ft. 5½-in. personality who has brought unbridled sex appeal back to the movies. A loud sustained wolf whistle has risen from the nation's barbershops and garages because of her now historic calendar pose, in which she lies nude on red velvet. Uneasy studio executives begged her last January to deny the story. But Marilyn believes in doing what comes naturally. She admitted she posed for the picture back in 1949 to pay her overdue rent. Asked if she really had nothing on in the photo, Marilyn, her blue eyes wide, purred: "I had the radio on." **AUG. 11, 1952**

BANANAS AND GIN

When his plane crashed on safari in Africa and he was believed dead, **Ernest Hemingway** walked out of the jungle carrying a bunch of bananas and a bottle of gin, saying: "My luck, she is running very good." **DEC. 13, 1954**

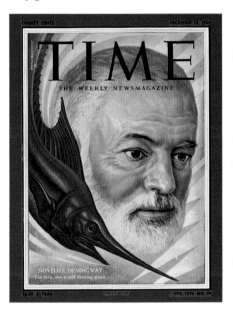

"LORD BYRON FROM BROOKLYN"

Marlon Brando has a nose that drips down his face, according to a make-up man, "like melted ice cream" (it caused him to flunk his first screen test ten years ago). But then again, as one fan tried to explain, he does have a kind of "lyric lunkishness—he looks like Lord Byron from Brooklyn." At moments he can vanish into the character he is portraying like a salamander into stone. **OCT. 11, 1954**

CARNATIONS AWAY!

The U.S. liner *Constitution* hove to off the port of Monaco one morning last week and set Hollywood's **Grace Kelly** aboard *Deo Juvante II*, the virginal white yacht of Grace's groom-to-be, **Prince Rainier III**. All Monaco broke loose. Rockets zoomed, sirens screamed, trolleys klaxoned. Overhead a seaplane belonging to Sea Lord Aristotle Onassis bombarded the couple with carnations. **APRIL 23, 1956**

THE NEW EVANGELIST

Before **Billy Graham** begins his sermon, he asks the audience to join him in a prayer. Then he plunges right into his text. He picks up the Bible again and again, swinging it, slamming it, almost literally hurling it at the Devil. Under the bright lights, he paces his rubber-matted platform, crouching, pointing, swooping upon his acres of audience from one angle, then another, his plangent voice hammering them with hardly a change of pace. **OCT. 25, 1954**

LONG LIVE THE QUEEN-TO-BE!

For the first time in 66 years, a reigning Queen opened Britain's Parliament. Like Victoria at her first Parliament, **Elizabeth II** has not yet been crowned. Her crown was borne before her on a crimson cushion by the Marquess of Salisbury; a coronet of diamonds and pearls took the crown's place on her brow. **NOV. 17, 1952**

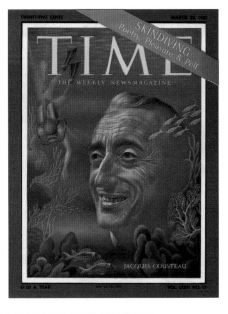

WITNESS Henry Grunwald on Ava Gardner

While I was visiting Hollywood [as a young TIME writer], correspondent Jim Murray and I took Ava Gardner to dinner at an Italian restaurant. An MGM press agent, George Nichols, insisted on joining us, presumably to see that Ava behaved herself. He was only partly successful. She spoke freely about her reputation as a sexpot—well deserved, she insisted. "People think I am the type who would take the busboy out back," she said, eyeing our young waiter. "Well, I just might." The waiter blushed till his face almost matched the spaghetti sauce.

"Fantastic," I said. Nichols tried to change the subject. Ava became increasingly irritated with him. She winked at me and announced she was going to the john. I excused myself to do the same. Without exchanging a word, we headed out of the restaurant and into her car. She was the most reckless driver I have ever known, but after a hair-raising ride, we arrived at her home and proceeded to attack a bottle of Courvoisier. She had just kicked off her shoes and started dancing slowly on the coffee table (Grunwald: "Fantastic!") when Nichols arrived, panting and fuming ... Ava never did finish her dance. **—Henry Grunwald**

POET OF THE DEPTHS

As any skindiver will readily admit, his sport is almost the singlehanded creation of a lean, visionary Frenchman named **Jacques-Yves Cousteau.** He is, all in one, its pioneer, foremost promoter, prophet and poet. **MARCH 28, 1960**

REVOLUTION

The civil rights movement
and the Vietnam War sparked
an unprecedented upheaval
in politics, culture and mores

National Guardsmen amid blazing ruins
in Detroit in 1967, where riots in the
black neighborhoods were the most
severe of the 1960s

Eric Pooley

A QUESTION OF AUTHORITY

The tumult of the time assaulted America's social stability

BULL CONNOR THOUGHT HE KNEW A THING OR TWO ABOUT POWER. IN MAY 1963 the public-safety commissioner of Birmingham, Ala., was ready to use water cannons and attack dogs on a group of civil rights demonstrators led by the Rev. Martin Luther King Jr. The protesters reacted in a way Connor found hard to fathom—they knelt in the street and prayed. "Let them turn their water on," said one. "Let them use their dogs. We are not leaving. Forgive them." Connor gave the order to mow down the marchers, and television beamed the scene to a horrified world. Among the viewers was President John F. Kennedy: he was so appalled that after two years of foot dragging he suddenly threw his weight behind a federal civil rights bill.

The blacks of Birmingham raised the fundamental question of the 1960s: Who has authority, and why? Six months later, the question was posed again in Dallas, when the squeeze of a trigger snuffed out the life of the world's most powerful man—the ultimate attack on authority. Kennedy's assassination began a nightmarish string that ended with the 1968 slayings of King and Robert Kennedy. Great leaders were called, great leaders were murdered, and great cities burned, baby, burned. Through it all, Vietnam was blazing too, an unwinnable, unfathomable, undeclared war that claimed 57,605 American lives in exchange for—what? The country never found out.

No wonder the young hitched a ride to another

America: a sweet-smelling place of laughter and music and bad poetry, where a sugar cube under the tongue could demolish the authority of reason itself. The prankster visions of the Acid Tests swirled around the stark realities of American power, and the decade found its signature moments: a flower in a gun barrel, a Defense Secretary scowling out a Pentagon window at the hippies trying to levitate his fortress. When Lyndon Johnson announced that he would not seek re-election, in March 1968, he was tacitly admitting that the freaks might be right.

BEFORE THE '60S, AMERICANS SEEMED IMMUNE TO THE REVOLUTIONARY impulse that defined the 20th century elsewhere. Periods of tumult— the giddy swirl of the '20s, the grinding despair of the Great Depres-

sion, which led so many to question capitalism itself—only served to highlight the broad, deep social stability born of American affluence. But the 1960s brought one great revolution to life in America—civil rights—and many smaller ones. Religious dogma, journalistic objectivity, middle-class morality—all came under assault as the war sputtered on. Pleasures were now political statements; student opposition to the war turned into an assault on Amerika. By 1970, when four students at Kent State were killed by National Guardsmen, Abbie Hoffman's "revolution for the hell of it" seemed nothing like revolution and an awful lot like hell. Recoiling, voters rejected the vaguely countercultural George McGovern in favor of four more years with Nixon. That set the stage for the apogee of public disillusionment, Watergate, and the Reagan Revolution, which blamed the '60s for the social pathologies afflicting America. Lasting dominion over the decade belonged to Madison Avenue, which turned the counterculture into the marketing tool it is today. Jerry Garcia is dead. Long live Cherry Garcia. ■

A LAST FAREWELL

The pallbearers, their white-gloved hands moving in careful precision, folded to a tight triangle the flag that had covered Kennedy's coffin for two days. Jackie took it and, hugging it to her breast, took a taper and lighted a blue flame at the foot of the grave—an "eternal light." Bobby and Teddy Kennedy touched taper to flame too, then they turned to go, and the funeral of John Kennedy was over.

That night, while the flame flickered in the dark over heaps of wreaths and flowers and a litter of film wrappings, crumpled bags and rolls of TV cable, Jackie Kennedy returned to the grave with Bobby. She put a small bouquet of lilies on the grave, prayed, wept, and went away. **DEC. 9, 1963**

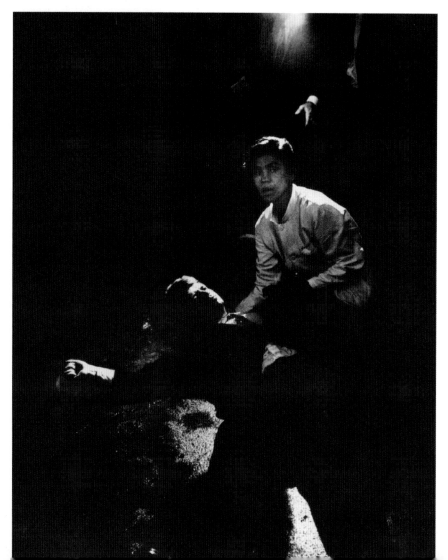

CRIME

TRAGEDY'S GRIP

The circumstances were cruel enough: son of a house already in tragedy's grip, father of ten with the eleventh expected, symbol of the youth and toughness, the wealth and idealism of the nation he sought to lead—this protean figure cut down by a small gun in a small cause. Crueler still, perhaps, was the absence of real surprise.

It was the unspoken expectation of the veteran campaigners who traveled with Robert Fitzgerald Kennedy that death was always somewhere out there in the crowd. **JUNE 14, 1968**

CIVIL RIGHTS

VOTING WITH THEIR FEET

Despite great gains in the past decade, the American Negro is still often denied the most basic right of citizenship under constitutional government—the right to vote. Last week [as protesters marched in Selma, Ala.] the Negro's struggle to achieve that right exploded into an orgy of police brutality, of clubs and whips and tear gas, of murder, of protests and parades and sit-ins in scores of U.S. cities and in the White House itself ... It was a very trying week for the foremost leader of the civil rights movement, Martin Luther King Jr. **MARCH 19, 1965**

CIVIL RIGHTS

BIRMINGHAM BOILS OVER

Birmingham Negroes had always been a docile lot. Downtown at night, they slouched in gloomy huddles beneath street lamps, talking softly. They knew their place: they were "niggers" in a Jim Crow town, and they bore the degradation in silence. Last week they smashed that image forever. The scenes were unforgettable. There was the Negro youth, sprawled on his back and spinning across the pavement, while firemen battered him with streams of water that could strip bark off trees. **MAY 17, 1963**

95

VIET NAM

A NEW KIND OF WAR

Everywhere South Viet Nam bustles with the U.S. presence ... Wave upon wave of combat-booted Americans—lean, laconic and looking for a fight—pour ashore from armadas of troopships. Day and night, screaming jets and prowling helicopters seek out the enemy from their swampy strongholds ... The Viet Cong's once-cocky hunters have become the cowering hunted as the cutting edge of U.S. fire power slashes into the thickets of Communist strength. If the U.S. has not yet won guaranteed certain victory in South Viet Nam, it has nonetheless undeniably averted certain defeat. As one top-ranking U.S. officer put it: "We've stemmed the tide."   **OCT. 22, 1965**

VICTORS? By 1966, images like Larry Burrows' picture of distraught U.S. troops were belying TIME's optimistic forecast [above] in 1965

DEMENTIA IN THE SECOND CITY

The assault from the left was furious, fluky and bizarre. Yet the Chicago police department responded in a way that could only be characterized as sanctioned mayhem. With billy clubs, tear gas and Mace, the blue-helmeted cops violated the civil rights of countless innocent citizens and contravened every accepted code of professional police discipline ...

No one could accuse the Chicago cops of discrimination. They savagely attacked hippies, yippies, New Leftists, revolutionaries, dissident Democrats, newsmen, photographers, passers-by, clergymen and at least one cripple ...

Foolhardy and arrogant as their tactics often were, the main goal of the protesters was to express their rejection of both the war and party bossism. Ironically—and perhaps most significantly—the demonstrators' most effective allies were the police, without whose brutal aid the protest would not have been so striking.   **SEPT. 6, 1968**

MARTYRDOM

It took half a century to transform Kent State from an obscure teachers college into the second largest university in Ohio, with 21,000 students and an impressive array of modern buildings on its main campus. But it took less than ten terrifying seconds last week to convert the traditionally conformist campus into a bloodstained symbol of the rising student rebellion against the Nixon Administration and the war in Southeast Asia. When National Guardsmen fired indiscriminately into a crowd of unarmed civilians, killing four students, the bullets wounded the nation.   **MAY 18, 1970**

DIPLOMACY

CAMARADERIE

There is a banquet at night. While Americans watching on television get the idea that it is some kind of folk festival, it is not quite so hearty. The huge Great Hall of the People engulfs the guests, much like China itself. Nixon is a dim figure with Chou En-lai, nibbling at his shark's fin dish. Pat's red dress is a drop of warm blood in the gray.

The toasts are a traditional exercise and Nixon makes the most of it. Seized by this emotional moment, Nixon visits each of the top tables, toasting each Chinese official with a clink, a touch of his glass to his lips. For the Americans there, it is a moving moment. There is the suspicion that the Chinese like it too. But who really knows? The night and the silence swallow everybody again. The visitors go back to their hotels in buses, a thin moon shining through the cold.   **MARCH 6, 1972**

CHINA

THE SCORPION DANCE

Chinese fought Chinese in the cities, and the ubiquitous *tatzebao*, or posters, attacked with such catholic ferocity—condemning both Mao's enemies and his lieutenants—that there may soon be no one left undenounced in all of Red China. To many observers in both the West and the East, it seemed as if China were reaching the final stages of the legendary dance of the scorpion—just before it stings itself to death.   **JAN. 13, 1967**

BERLIN

THE WALL

Even as the 80,000 East German *Volkspolizei* (People's Police) and *Volksarmee* (People's Army) troops were erecting their barricades across most of the 80 border-transit points last week, desperate clusters of East Berliners were still trying to break out to freedom ... After a helmeted *Vopo* guard at the new barrier leaped across the barbed wire and escaped to the West, East German officers began keeping their enlisted men several yards from the wire to prevent more defections.   **AUG. 25, 1961**

MAN OF THE YEAR 1961–1972

1961 Overcoming the doubters who said he was too young—or that a Roman Catholic could not be elected President—43-year-old **John F. Kennedy** fought a tough battle against the G.O.P.'s Richard Nixon and won the White House in a squeaker.

1962 Pope John XXIII "opened the windows" of his age-old Church and sparked a revolution.

1963 Arming his troops with dreams and oratory, **Martin Luther King Jr.** led the civil rights cause.

1964 After a landslide victory over Goldwater, **Lyndon Johnson** began to forge his Great Society.

1965 Overseeing the struggling U.S. "grunts" in Vietnam was **Gen. William Westmoreland.**

1966 Salad days: kids **25 and Under** were shaking up society—and trusting no one over 30.

1967 Vietnam turned **Lyndon Johnson** from architect of social reform into an embattled Lear.

1968 As America's race to the moon entered its last lap, TIME hailed the **Apollo Astronauts**.

1969 Behind Richard Nixon's successful race for the White House: **The Middle Americans.**

1970 West Germany's **Willy Brandt** gambled on "Ostpolitik," a new dialogue with the East.

1971 Richard Nixon opened China's door, devalued the dollar and quelled antiwar protest.

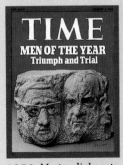

1972 Master diplomats **Kissinger and Nixon** talked détente with the U.S.S.R. and visited Mao.

SPACE

TOWARD THE MOON

Astronauts James A. McDivitt and Edward H. White II in their 62-orbit Gemini 4 flight ... showed that man can endure in space. Not only did White spend 20 minutes floating alone outside the capsule, but as a bonus the space twins returned to earth with a breathtakingly brilliant series of films of the space stroll. **JUNE 18, 1965**

SPACE

IN SECOND PLACE

For an endless, heart-stopping moment, the tall, slim rocket hung motionless—incredibly balanced above its incandescent tail. Slowly it climbed the sky, outracing the racket of its engine as it screamed toward space. In the returning silence, the amplified thump of an electronic timer beat like a pulse across the sands of Florida's Cape Canaveral. The pulse of the nation beat with it. Riding that long white missile as it soared aloft last week was Navy Commander Alan B. Shepard Jr., first U.S. astronaut ever fired into space. And riding with him was his country's pride, the prestige of his country's science, the promise of his country's future on the expanding frontiers of the universe ...

Though his capsule ... curved along its course with infinite precision, its ballistic trajectory could not be compared with the far more complicated orbital flight of Russia's Yuri Gagarin last month.   **MAY 12, 1961**

1961 Yuri Gagarin, Soviet hero and the first man in space, "thought of the motherland" in orbit.

1961 "Few men in history have been watched over so carefully" as first U.S. astronaut **Alan Shepard.**

1962 John Glenn was "incredibly matter-of-fact" when facing peril on the first U.S. orbital mission.

WITNESS   Hugh Sidey on John F. Kennedy

John Glenn was floating back down to earth after becoming the first astronaut to orbit the planet. Along with the other White House correspondents, I was waiting for the President's statement when I was suddenly summoned to the Oval Office. I was jubilant, believing Kennedy was going to reward me for TIME's interest in space with an exclusive view of him talking by phone to Glenn.

But as the door of the office swung open, I saw Kennedy behind his desk with a dark face reading TIME. "Where'd you get this story about me posing for the cover of *Gentlemen's Quarterly*? It's all a lie."

I really did not know anything about the story, I stammered, but would find out. He blew up, got red in the face, threw the magazine down, ranted about how we were out to destroy him, then marched around his desk and shook his fist in my face. "People remember other people for one thing," he ranted on. "They remember Calvin Coolidge for wearing an Indian headdress ... They will remember me for posing for a clothing magazine." Just then Glenn came on the line. Kennedy's whole demeanor changed. With a lilting, joyous tone, he shouted his greetings. After five minutes of congratulations and chitchat, he gave the phone back, stalked back to me and resumed the attack.   —Hugh Sidey

1969 Neil Armstrong: "a ghostly, white-clad figure ... testing a new environment for man."

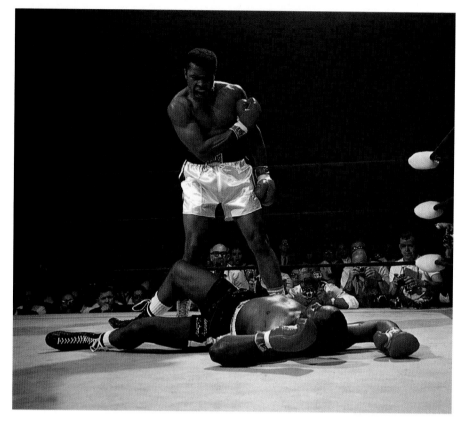

SPORT

THE ANCHOR PUNCH

Most of the fans in the arena had not seen the knockout punch [that brought Cassius Clay victory over Sonny Liston in their second championship fight]; neither had the 500,000 others watching on closed-circuit TV. "Fix! Fix! Fix!" they chanted. "Fake! Fake! Fake!" ... Even Cassius was confused. "I think I hit him with a left hook and a right cross," he said. "But I want to see the video tape."

When he saw the tape, Cassius had a new story. The punch that flattened Liston, he insisted, was his secret "anchor punch"—so named because it anchors opponents to the floor. Said Clay: "It's a chop, so fast you can't see it. It's karate. It's got a twist to it. Just one does the job."

JUNE 4, 1965

ESSAY

DIFFERENT DRUMMER

What took place on the days and nights of Aug. 15 through 17, 1969, on the 600-acre farm of Max Yasgur in Bethel, N.Y., ostensibly, was the Woodstock Music and Art Fair, which was billed as "An Aquarian Exposition" of music and peace. It was that and more—much more. The festival turned out to be history's largest happening. As the moment when the special culture of U.S. youth of the '60s openly displayed its strength, appeal and power, it may rank as one of the significant political and sociological events of the age.

Thousands of young people, who had previously thought of themselves as part of an isolated minority, experienced the euphoric sense of discovering that they are, as the saying goes, what's happening. Adults were made more aware than ever before that the children of the welfare state and the atom bomb do indeed march to the beat of a different drummer, as well as to the tune of an electric guitarist.   **AUG. 29, 1969**

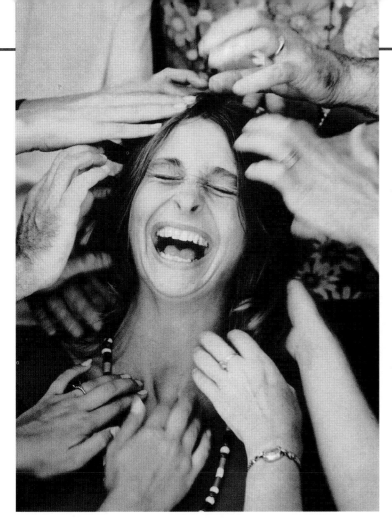

TOUCH ME, HEAL ME

The encounter group, as it evolved at the Esalen Institute, is first of all a vehicle to provide an intense emotional experience. It is usually kept small enough—half a dozen to 20 members—to generate intimate response ... To the uninitiated, it can be a shocking experience. As TIME's Andrea Svedberg, who attended one, reports: "People touch, hold hands, kiss, throw each other up in the air, fight, use all the dirty words, tell each other cruel truths. Every aspect of so-called proper behavior is discarded. Every emotion is out in the open—everyone's property." Feelings are not spared. In time, the group develops a tribal loyalty, as fiercely protective as it is critical. **NOV. 9, 1970**

MUSIC

BLUES FOR JANIS

The quart bottle of Southern Comfort that she held aloft onstage was at once a symbol of her load and a way of lightening it ... Purists insist that no white man or woman can really sing the blues, because they cannot have known the pain of body and soul from which true blues rise. In her music, Janis Joplin certainly came as close to authentic blues as any white singer ever has. **OCT. 19, 1970**

MUSIC

ALL RIGHT?

Ray Charles lives in a world of sounds alone, and even his best songs do not completely tell what goes on there. Something else remains—the catch in the way he sings "That's all right"—and it suggests that something is wrong. How can it be all right, when it stirs the listener so sadly? **MAY 10, 1963**

CINEMA
TOO MUCH REHEARSAL?

Richard Burton staggers around … like a man who suddenly realizes that he has lost his script and is really reading some old sides from *King of Kings.* In the big love scenes "the ne'er-lust-wearied Antony" seems strangely bored—as if perhaps he had rehearsed too much. As for Taylor … she screeches like a ward heeler's wife at a block party. **JUNE 21, 1963**

PAINTING
MISSING PERSON

Stockholm's classy Moderna Museet knocked itself blue putting on a giant show celebrating American Popinjay Andy Warhol, 36. This earned the supreme tribute—an appearance by the artist himself, with his clownish protégée, Viva, in town and cutting up for photographers. "I was going to send someone that looked like me," said Warhol. "It worked once before." So it did, just three weeks ago, in fact, when Warhol without notice sent a buddy named Alan Midgette to impersonate him in a lecture tour of Western colleges. The ruse wasn't uncovered until someone in Oregon thought to call Andy in New York. **MARCH 1, 1968**

MUSIC
NEW FACE OF FOLK

All over the U.S., folk singers are doing what folk singers are classically supposed to do—singing about current crises. Not since the Civil War era have they done so with such intensity. Instead of keening over the poor old cowpoke who died in the streets of Laredo or chronicling the life cycle of the blue-tailed fly … they are singing about police dogs and racial murder … the Peter, Paul and Mary recording of Bob Dylan's *Blowin' in the Wind* is the fastest selling single Warner Bros. Records has ever cut. **JULY 19, 1963**

DEMON OF DEATH VALLEY

Among the rattlesnakes of Death Valley, **Charles Manson** and his retinue holed up in run-down cabins and led an indolent, almost savage existence, singing Manson's songs, dancing, stealing cars for cash, picking through garbage for food.   **DEC. 12, 1969**

SECRETS OF THE FAB FOUR

At 1:20 p.m. the jetliner touched down at Kennedy Airport, and the whole place went up for grabs. Some 2,000 hooky-playing, caterwauling teenagers stomped, whistled, screamed, sang or just plain fainted while the plane slowly disgorged 105 passengers, 11 crew members and four British Beetles. Oops, **Beatles.** What was their secret? A good press agent, chirped Ringo Starr. (They have 17.)   **FEB. 14, 1964**

HEIGHT OF NONCHALANCE

Barbra Streisand was invited to Washington to sing for President Kennedy. Her opening line to him was: "You're a doll." When he inquired politely how long she had been singing, she said: "As long as you've been President."   **APRIL 10, 1964**

THE PEOPLE'S POPE

When **Jacqueline Kennedy** came to visit, **Pope John XXIII** asked his secretary how to address her. The reply: "'Mrs. Kennedy,' or just 'Madame,' since she is of French origin and has lived in France." Waiting in his private library, the Pope mumbled: "Mrs. Kennedy, Madame; Madame, Mrs. Kennedy." Then the doors opened on the U.S. First Lady and he stood up, extended his arms and cried: "Jacqueline!" **JAN. 4, 1963**

NOTES FROM THE UNDERGROUND

Last week Guerrilla Leader **Yasser Arafat** discussed the war with TIME's Gavin Scott in a cave on the Israeli border, from which he was directing fedayeen operations. Scott cabled: "Arafat sat at a wooden desk studying military reports by the light of a gas lamp. Machine guns were stacked in a corner." Arafat introduced Scott to a 13-year-old commando, who, he said, had already been on 14 operations. **MARCH 30, 1970**

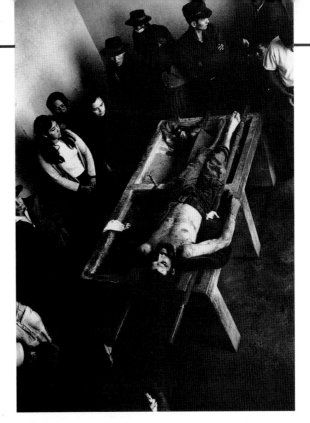

END OF A LEGEND

Che Guevara caught a bullet in his left thigh as he advanced toward the government troops; another bullet knocked his M-1 carbine right out of his hands. In Che's rucksack, the Bolivian Rangers found a book entitled *Essays in Contemporary Capitalism*, several codes, two war diaries ... **OCT. 20, 1967**

ENCORE!

Rudolf Nureyev was the man of the hour and he relished every minute of it. At a post-performance party, he exuberantly danced the watusi and the frug with partner **Margot Fonteyn**, soundly bussed one of the pretty girls from the corps de ballet. His favorite restaurant—the Russian Tea Room—was packed with fans hoping to catch a glimpse of him in his turtleneck sweater and low-cut boots. **APRIL 30, 1965**

WHAT, NO FOOD COLORING?

With her next volume on French cooking taking up all her time, **Julia Child** has stopped taping *The French Chef*, plans to wait until color comes to educational TV before resuming it because, "I'm tired of gray food." **NOV. 25, 1966**

BOWING OUT

August 1974: defying his
fate as the first President
to resign, Richard Nixon
flashes a victory sign as
he departs the White House

LIMITS

Morally, politically, militarily, diplomatically—and almost literally—the U.S. just ran out of gas

Richard Lacayo

THE CAN'T-DO MENTALITY

In the '70s, doubts began to darken the nation's psyche

THE QUINTESSENTIAL IMAGE OF WORLD WAR II WAS THE FLAG RAISING AT IWO Jima. For Vietnam, it was a helicopter scrambling off the U.S. embassy roof in Saigon. Apocalypse Then: the chaotic endgame of the Vietnam War fatally charged the atmosphere of the 1970s, a decade in which America discovered limits to its power and wealth. For a nation long accustomed to expansion—material, geographic and psychological—this was something new and unwelcome. Only the Great Depression—an appropriate name—had presented a comparable challenge to national optimism, and that was followed by the reassuring wartime victory and postwar boom. In the '70s that boom gave way to a different explosion:

in oil prices, interest rates and inflation, OPEC would prove to have powers NATO could only dream of. Even the environmental movement would sound a warning: air and water, the fundamentals of life, were in limited supply. In short, in the '70s America downsized its expectations. Out with Pax Americana. In with the Vietnam Syndrome. Out with the Cadillac. In with the Toyota. But first, out with the President, via Watergate; nearly two years spent sifting through the rubble of Richard Nixon. The hopes of a clean start raised by Gerald Ford collapsed under the Nixon pardon and an economic crisis as impervious to Ford's WHIP INFLATION NOW buttons as it had been to Nixon's wage-and-price controls.

It was Jimmy Carter's greatest asset that he was a new face; he offered the promise of accountability in Washington and an end to Henry Kissinger's secretive realpolitik abroad. He got mixed results at home. So in the same way that Nixon found a legacy in his opening to

China, Carter turned to the Panama Canal treaties and the Camp David peace accords. Both were milestones typical of the era. In one, the U.S. agreed to give up a prime keepsake of its earlier expansion; in the other, it mediated where it was powerless to dictate.

BUT THIS AGE OF LIMITS WAS STILL IN SOME RESPECTS an age of exploration. The '70s were when the '60s hit home. Head shops came to suburbia. Mom took yoga. And there were days when all the world was *Oh! Calcutta!* As experiments do, some ended in disaster, some in the cheesy solipsisms of the Me decade. All the same, by the simple pressure of new possibilities, lives were refashioned, and not just into life-styles. Women, gays, blacks all decided to take seriously that stuff about

the pursuit of happiness. Every week, when Mary Tyler Moore threw her hat into the air, a lot of people knew exactly how she felt. Seen in that forgiving light, even the sheer awfulness of '70s taste—leisure suits in grape-jelly purple, shag-carpeted vans, KC and the Sunshine Band—was just an unconfined democratic impulse set loose in the marketplace.

But something else had been set loose too. Patty Hearst, Jonestown, Squeaky Fromme—every year seemed to produce some weird episode that hinted at a deeper instability. By 1979, when the Soviet Union invaded Afghanistan and Iranian students seized the U.S. embassy in Tehran—another embassy, another scene of humiliation—there was a feeling in the air that change must come. Let the record show that in his famous speech on the somber national mood, Jimmy Carter never spoke the word malaise. By that time, he didn't need to. ∎

THE PRESIDENT SHOULD RESIGN

[In the only editorial ever to appear in TIME, *Managing Editor Henry Grunwald called on Richard Nixon to step down over Watergate.]* Richard Nixon and the nation have passed a tragic point of no return. It now seems likely that the President will have to give up his office: he has irredeemably lost his moral authority, the confidence of most of the country, and therefore his ability to govern effectively. **NOV. 12, 1973**

BITTER END: On Aug. 9, 1974, Richard Nixon formally resigns, top left; as his helicopter departs the White House, Gerald and Betty Ford take the reins, above

DEATH IN JONESTOWN

"The large central building was ringed by bright colors. It looked like a parking lot filled with cars. When the plane dipped lower, the cars turned out to be bodies. Scores and scores of bodies—hundreds of bodies—wearing red dresses, blue T shirts, pink slacks, children's polka-dotted jumpers. Couples with their arms around each other, children holding parents. Nothing moved. Washing hung on the clotheslines. But nothing moved."

So reported TIME's Donald Neff, one of the first newsmen to fly into the obscure hamlet of Jonestown in Guyana [where] some 900 members of the California-based Peoples Temple died in a self-imposed ritual of mass suicide. **DEC. 4, 1978**

THE HEARST NIGHTMARE

Only three months ago, Patty Hearst was a quiet, comely heiress to a famed publishing fortune ... Kidnapped on Feb. 4 by an obscure revolutionary band that calls itself the Symbionese Liberation Army, but is more of a ragtag platoon, she seemed close to release two weeks ago .... Then she stunned her family and friends by announcing that she had joined her abductors and adopted the name Tania, after the German-Argentine mistress of Latin American Revolutionary Che Guevara. Whether through conversion or coercion, she emerged last week as a foul-mouthed bank robber ... Her anguished father Randolph A. Hearst exclaimed: "It's terrible! Sixty days ago, she was a lovely child. Now there's a picture of her in a bank with a gun in her hand." **APRIL 29, 1974**

IRAN

BLACKMAILING THE U.S.

It was an ugly, shocking image of innocence and impotence, of tyranny and terror, of madness and mob rule. Blindfolded and bound, employees of the U.S. embassy in Tehran were paraded last week before vengeful crowds while their youthful captors gloated and jeered. On a gray Sunday morning, students invoking the name of Iran's Ayatullah Ruhollah Khomeini invaded the embassy, overwhelmed its Marine Corps guards and took some 60 Americans as hostages. Their demand: surrender the deposed Shah of Iran ... as the price of the Americans' release. While flatly refusing to submit to such outrageous blackmail, the U.S. was all but powerless to free the victims. As the days passed, nerves became more frayed and the crisis deepened. So far as was known, the hostages had been humiliated but not harmed, yet with demonstrators chanting "Death to America" outside the compound, there was no way to guarantee that the event would not have a violent ending. Meanwhile, a wave of anger spread across the U.S. On campuses, Iranian flags were torched ...   **NOV. 19, 1979**

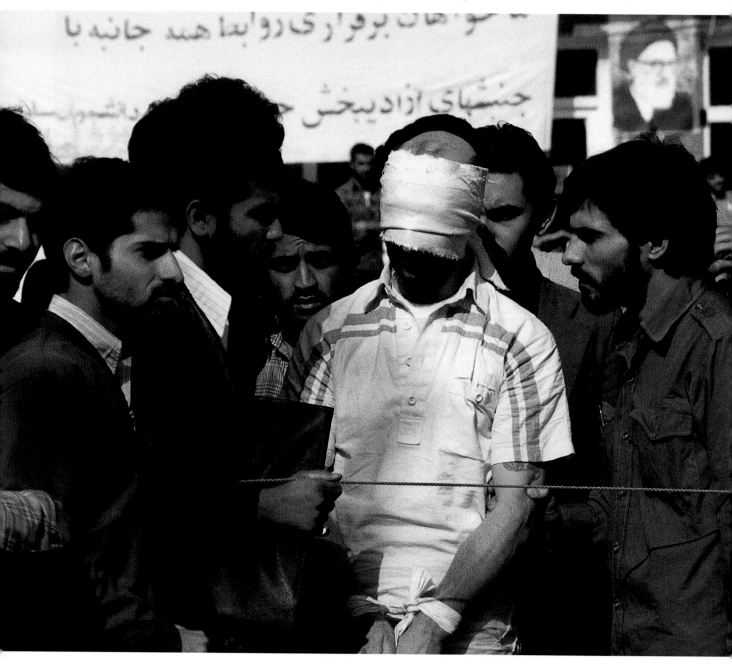

A VISION OF PEACE

After 13 days of being cloistered with their closest aides at Camp David, President Jimmy Carter, Egyptian President Anwar Sadat and Israeli Premier Menachem Begin emerged [with] two documents that were giant steps toward peace in the Middle East ... In an emotional piece of theater, Begin walked behind Carter to Sadat, and the two men embraced, not once but twice. **SEPT. 25, 1978**

CAMBODIA

CAVALCADE OF DEATH

It is a country soaked in blood, devastated by war, and its people are starving to death. Every day numbed witnesses to the appalling tragedy that has consumed Cambodia trek across the border into Thailand. Stumbling on reed-thin legs through the high elephant grass, they form a grisly cavalcade of specters, wrapped in black rags. **NOV. 12, 1979**

THE SEXES

A WATERSHED FOR WOMEN

The battle was over—and to the curators went the spoils. The lectern emblem proclaiming NATIONAL WOMEN'S CONFERENCE 1977, which had hung for three hectic, fractious, exhilarating days in Houston, last week was headed for the Smithsonian Institution. It will repose with such other memorabilia as the star-spangled banner that flew over Fort McHenry. And well it might. Over a weekend and a day, American women had reached some kind of watershed in their own history, and that of the nation ...

Peggy Kokernot, 25, a runner [at center of the picture above] wants a women's marathon at the Olympics ... But the International Olympic Committee recently turned down a proposal for even a 3,000-meter (roughly two miles) women's race. The distance, presumably, is too exhausting for the "weaker sex." **DEC. 5, 1977**

LIVING

THE EPIDERMIS EPIDEMIC

With astonishing swiftness, streaking, the art of the point-to-point dash in the buff, has burgeoned into an unabashed, unclad fad. On busy U.S. Route 1, traffic was brought to a cheerful standstill by 533 University of Maryland students chain-dancing *au naturel*. **MARCH 18, 1974**

RELIGION

JOHN PAUL, SUPERSTAR

As he led his triumphant seven-day journey of joy through the U.S., Pope John Paul II confirmed what his earlier tours of Mexico and Poland had intimated: after only a year in office, the Pontiff is emerging as the kind of incandescent leader that the world so hungers for—one who can make people feel that they have been lifted above the drabness of their own lives, and can show them that they are capable of better emotions, and better deeds, than they may have thought … When the Pope said Mass on a 180-acre pasture in Iowa, the throng totaled 350,000. A Protestant minister turned to his Catholic neighbor, Joe Hays, and said: "You got a Pope who knows how to pope." **OCT. 15, 1979**

1972 Before terrorists struck, **Mark Spitz** plowed to a record seven gold medals at Munich.

1976 Skating with "*élan* and musicality," **Dorothy Hamill** took the gold at Innsbruck.

1976 "An infinitely solemn wisp of a girl," **Nadia Comaneci** scored perfect 10s in Montreal.

1980 Speedy siblings **Eric and Beth Heiden** were the poster kids for the Lake Placid Games.

ENERGY

A NUCLEAR NIGHTMARE

Suddenly, at 4 a.m., alarm lights blinked red on the instrument panels. A siren whooped a warning. In the understated jargon of the nuclear power industry, an "event" had occurred. In plain English, it was the beginning of the worst accident in the history of U.S. nuclear power, and of a long, often confused nightmare that threw the future of the nuclear industry into question. There was no panic at the plant, called Three Mile Island ...   **APRIL 9, 1979**

ENERGY

OPEC'S GAMBIT

In every car and tractor, in every tank and plane—oil. Behind every lighted glass tower, giant industrial plant or little workshop, computer and moon rocket and television signal—oil. Behind fertilizers, drugs, chemicals—the same substance that until recently was taken for granted as a seemingly inexhaustible and obedient treasure. Few noted the considerable historic irony that the world's most advanced civilizations depended for this treasure on countries generally considered, weak, compliant and disunited. **JAN. 6, 1975**

MAN OF THE YEAR 1973-1979

1973 Pursuing truth into the Oval Office, **Judge John Sirica** broke Watergate open.

1974 **King Faisal** of Saudi Arabia led the OPEC price hikes that roiled world markets.

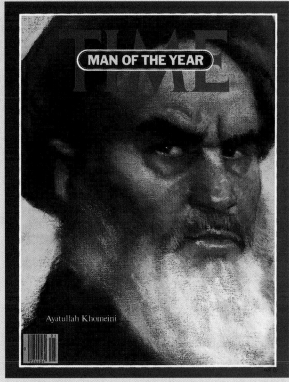

Ayatullah Khomeini

1975 Hear me roar! Refusing to play second-best, **American Women** asserted their equality.

1976 **Jimmy Carter** parlayed his outsider status into a successful run for the White House.

1979 When TIME named Iran's leader **Ayatullah Khomeini** Man of the Year, even as Iran held U.S. hostages, 14,081 readers wrote to protest. The editors explained that the designation did not honor Khomeini but reflected the significance of his deeds.

WITNESS John Stacks on Chief Justice Warren Burger

Working from a leak from the Supreme Court, the magazine published an account of the landmark *Roe v. Wade* abortion-rights decision just as the court announced it. Warren Burger, who was then Chief Justice, was infuriated and demanded a meeting with TIME's editors. A group of them, including editor-in-chief Hedley Donovan, came down from New York to the Washington bureau, where I was then news editor, and we arranged a dinner in the bureau's offices on 16th Street.

Throughout the meal, Burger argued that it was unconscionable to scoop the court, that using information from clerks, who he assumed were the source of our story, was tantamount to wiretapping the Supreme Court. Each time he launched into a new argument, he would consult a loose-leaf binder he had brought with him. In order to hide this from his dinner partners, he would rock his chair back and put his foot on the edge of our dining room table. And each time he rocked back, the Chief Justice of the United States advertised that he had neglected to zip up his fly.

We heard him out until Donovan said that he did not consider the scoop a breach and that we would continue to cover the court aggressively, good night. What Burger didn't know was that our source was one of his fellow Justices, who was angry with Burger for having held the decision from the previous fall to spare Richard Nixon political embarrassment. —*John Stacks*

1977 **Anwar Sadat** of Egypt dared greatly with a surprise peace gambit and a later trip to Israel.

1978 To a China long racked by extremism, **Teng Hsiao-p'ing** brought stability at last.

HALEY HITS HOME

For eight consecutive nights, tens of millions of Americans were riveted by ABC's epic dramatization of Alex Haley's *Roots* ... more than boffo TV, [it] was a social phenomenon, a potentially important benchmark in U.S. race relations.   **FEB. 14, 1977**

CINEMA

THE YEAR'S BEST MOVIE

Star Wars is a grand and glorious film ... a combination of *Flash Gordon, The Wizard of Oz,* the Errol Flynn swashbucklers of the '30s and '40s and almost every western ever screened ... [it] has brought fun back to the movies and glowingly demonstrated that they still can make 'em like they used to. **MAY 30, 1977**

CINEMA

LOVE AND LA-DE-DAH

Annie Hall [is] by far the best thing Woody Allen or Diane Keaton has ever done ... Does anyone doubt that young women across the country are looking into their mirrors and trying to find just the right intonation with which to murmur "La-de-dah"?   **SEPT. 26, 1977**

MUSIC

THE BOSS

Bruce Springsteen is not a golden California boy or a glitter queen from Britain. In his leather jacket and shredded undershirt, he is a glorified gutter rat from a dying New Jersey resort town who walks with an easy swagger that's part stage presence, part boardwalk braggadocio. His music is primal, in touch with all the impulses of wild humor and glancing melancholy, street tragedy and punk anarchy that have made rock the voice of a generation.   **OCT. 27, 1975**

ART
PLAIN AND FENCY

"I predict that artworks of the future will be in size category of Chinese Wall, and may become one day just as beautiful. To me, Chinese Wall is greatest artwork ever created by mankind." Thus said Artist Christo Javacheff (professional name: Christo) in his dense Bulgarian accent in 1968. Last week this prediction was coming true—more or less—as Christo's latest project, *Running Fence*, moved toward completion on the coast of Northern California. A shimmering construction of nylon slung between steel posts, [it consists of] 2,050 posts, 165,000 yds. of material, miles of wire and hundreds of thousands of hooks. Cost: $2,250,000. **SEPT. 20, 1976**

THEATER
DANCE OF LIFE

In *A Chorus Line* Michael Bennett, who may be a direct descendant of Terpsichore, has made dance a central theme as well as a supremely exhilarating act. The chorus line is his symbol of mass anonymity. It is also his symbol of teamwork, with the emphasis equally distributed between team and work. Behind the faceless mass, there is a face; behind the dazzling precision of the dance, there is a terrifying vulnerability … **JUNE 2, 1975**

121

FALLEN ANGEL

"I was a shy, ugly kid who led a big fantasy life," **Cher,** (christened Cherilyn), recalls. "I thought I was an angel from heaven sent to cure polio. When Dr. Salk did it, I was really pissed off." **MARCH 17, 1975**

AN ARTIST BECOMES AN EXILE

Last week began the exile of one of the world's great writers, an authentic hero in an age sorely lacking them, the man who has come to represent the conscience of Russia: **Alexander Solzhenitsyn**   **FEB. 25, 1974**

BALLET'S NEW IDOL

Less than a year since **Mikhail Baryshnikov** [defected], the public has made him a superstar and calls him by his nickname. A ticket outlet in Manhattan put up a sign saying, "Misha tickets sold out."   **MAY 19, 1975**

DISCOLAND'S RULING DYNASTY

When Victor Willis, lead singer of the **Village People,** spun himself off into a solo career, the thump-thump-thump that reverberates through Discoland, U.S.A., was suddenly muffled. After all, the flamboyant sextet is the ruling clan of that realm; they have made songs like *Macho Man* and *Y.M.C.A.* into nocturnal national anthems.   **SEPT. 3, 1979**

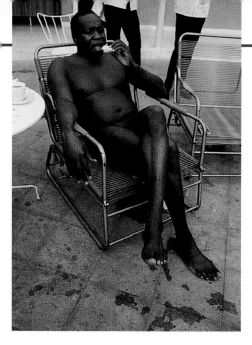

WILD MAN OF AFRICA

Uganda's porcine President-for-Life, Field Marshal **Idi Amin Dada,** 49, is both killer and clown, big-hearted buffoon and strutting martinet. He can be as playful as a kitten and as lethal as a lion. He stands 6 ft. 4 in. tall and carries a massive bulk of nearly 300 lbs., and within that girth courses the unharnessed ego of a small child, a craze for attention and reverence.   **MARCH 7, 1977**

BIRTH OF "THE BURN"

It may be the only gym that contributes profits to solar energy, tenants' rights and better housing. It could only be located in Beverly Hills, and the proprietress could only be **Jane Fonda** … on a clear day, Befores can see an ideal After: Fonda herself, at 41 a svelte mother of two, scissoring and sitting up.   **JULY 30, 1979**

HIGH STEPPIN' TO STARDOM

Check it out! Man walks down that street so fine. Strides easy. Arms arc … Smiling. Stepping so smart. Rolls, almost. Swings his butt like he's shifting gears in a swivel chair. Weight stays, sways in his hips. Shoulders, straight, shift with the strut. High and light. Street's all his, past doubt. It's all there in the walk that **John Travolta** takes through the opening credits of *Saturday Night Fever.*   **APRIL 3, 1978**

THE MUPPETS: MANIC MAGIC

After a take, **Miss Piggy** complained teasingly about "the man who is always following me around," referring to Muppeteer Frank Oz, and coyly peeked under the green flap at the bottom of Kermit's costume, exposing Jim Henson's arm. "Oh, you've got one too!"   **DEC. 25, 1978**

BUSTING OUT
On Nov. 10, 1989,
East Germans hailed
their new freedom
by smashing the
hated Berlin Wall

COMEBACK

In Reagan's Washington and on Gordon Gekko's Wall Street, it was a time of risk and reward. In the end, the payoffs were big

George J. Church

A TECTONIC SHIFT

Moscow collapsed under the staggering cost of the cold war

PERHAPS NEVER HAS THE MOOD OF A DECADE REVERSED ITSELF SO TOTALLY. THE 1980s began with the worst U.S. inflation in 60 years and a deepening dread of nuclear annihilation. As they closed, inflation was making a last and unsuccessful assault on an economy that had found new resources, the Berlin Wall was tumbling down, and the Soviet empire was dissolving. The cold war was over—*and the West won!* The road between was hardly a smooth climb. Ronald Reagan gave the U.S. a heady draft of optimism while reversing the direction of government policy, recasting social programs and cutting taxes. Unmatched by spending reductions, however, those cuts sent deficits soaring to unheard-of highs, and the double-digit inflation of 1980 was cured only by double-digit unemployment in 1982.

The economy revived, but an outsize share of the benefit seemed to flow to Wall Street. Mergers proliferated wildly, mostly, it seemed, for the enrichment of a few financial manipulators—novelist Tom Wolfe's Masters of the Universe. Moralists bemoaned what they saw as a sanctification of greed—not only in the U.S. but also in Margaret Thatcher's Britain, Helmut Kohl's West Germany and, of all places, Red China. But unlike in the irrationally exuberant 1920s, disaster did not strike. Though stocks fell even faster on Oct. 19, 1987, than they had in 1929, they bounced back higher than ever, setting the stage for the roaring bull market of the '90s. Something fundamental had happened to the boom-and-bust cycle that had charted the century.

Something fundamental was happening to communism as well. Reagan's 1982 prediction that it was headed for "the ash heap of history" was lost in a rising sea of angst, captured in a 1983 made-for-TV movie, *The Day After*, that dramatized the clinical horrors of a nuclear exchange. The U.S. and U.S.S.R. had broken off all arms-control negotiations and were arming rival sides in shooting wars in El Salvador and Nicaragua (whose anticommunist guerrillas would play a central role in the great Iran-*contra* scandal of the Reagan years).

BENEATH THE SURFACE, THOUGH, THE ALIGNMENT OF FORCES WAS SHIFTING. REAGAN'S BIG military buildup, and in particular his widely derided attempt to create a Star Wars antimissile defense, was putting heavy pressure on the Soviet Union to keep up. Moscow was vulnerable because the Soviet economy was decaying badly, and its leadership was nearly paralyzed. Only in 1985, after three Kremlin funerals in three years, did a leader, Mikhail Gorbachev, emerge who was realistic and vigorous enough to attempt drastic reforms.

In a sequence of summit meetings, Gorbachev and Reagan brought about the de-escalation of the arms race, which the Soviet leader realized was swallowing more resources than he could afford. The European satellites were too, so Gorbachev told their chiefs that Soviet tanks would no longer keep them in power. That started a chain reaction that left both sides dumbfounded. By the end of 1989, the Soviet bloc had dissolved: Poland, Hungary, Czechoslovakia, East Germany and Romania all installed noncommunist regimes. Even then, nobody would have guessed that in another two years the Soviet Union itself would shatter into 15 pieces. The world was entering a strange new era: only one super-power; no cold war. ■

INVESTIGATIONS
OLLIE'S TURN

The silence is over. The cameras are in place, the microphones tuned, the TV networks willing, even eager, to drop their soap operas and go live to Capitol Hill. This week, after seven months of claiming his Fifth Amendment privilege, Oliver North at last appears before the congressional committees probing the Iran-*contra* affair and begins to talk in public. **JULY 13, 1987**

THE PRESIDENCY
GIPPER'S QUIPS

When Nancy Reagan first arrived at the hospital, her wounded husband deadpanned, "Honey, I forgot to duck." Earlier, Reagan said to surgeons as he entered the operating room: "Please tell me you're Republicans." After the surgery, he wrote a note to his doctors: "Send me to L.A., where I can see the air I'm breathing." **APRIL 13, 1981**

1981 Ronald Reagan named fellow Westerner **Sandra Day O'Connor** to the Supreme Court.

1984 The Democrats' **Geraldine Ferraro** was the first woman to run on a national ticket.

THE HOSTAGES

AN END TO THE LONG ORDEAL

The freedom flight [out of Iran to Algiers] landed in a rainstorm. In the glare of television lights, Bruce Laingen, the chargé d'affaires at the Tehran embassy, led Kathryn Koob and Elizabeth Ann Swift, who wore the familiar yellow ribbons in their hair, down a ramp and into the arms of the normally undemonstrative Warren Christopher. [The former hostages] flashed victory signs and shouted: "Thank you! We made it!" **FEB. 2, 1981**

at was left of
search team
through the
, a head ap-
e arms and
the body of a
clad only in
aculously, he
. The lethal
estimated to
about 2,000
losives. The
r 30 ft. deep
CT. 31, 1983

1988 Olympic medalist **Jackie Joyner-Kersee** spearheaded a new era for women in athletics.

1989 As the revolution in their expectations continued, TIME helped **Women Face the '90s.**

POLAND

SOLIDARITY!

Six months ago, Lech Walesa was an unemployed electrician. Today, as leader of the Communist world's only independent labor union, he is one of the most powerful men in Poland, a folk hero not only to millions of his countrymen but to much of the world. His achievement all but defies description; in effect, he single-handed rallied his fellow workers to stand up against the will and the might of the Soviet Union. **DEC. 29, 1980**

NICARAGUA

JUNGLE WAR

The campaign of military pressure on Nicaragua continued to expand last week, and so did its potential for controversy. As part of a coordinated offensive, some 6,000 CIA-backed *contras* were marching from their Honduran base camps into the Nicaraguan interior. Simultaneously a 200-man *contra* column moved from the south to occupy a strategic hamlet on Nicaragua's isolated Caribbean coast, and gain a new military and political advantage after the most intense and sustained fighting of their hit-and-run guerrilla war ...

A *contra* assault column stormed into the settlement of San Juan del Norte, a remote Nicaraguan village of some 950 people. ... After a vigorous three-day firefight, the *contra* attackers succeeded in overrunning about 120 Sandinista defenders entrenched amid San Juan del Norte's thatched adobe huts. **APRIL 23, 1982**

CHINA

DESPAIR AND DEATH IN A BEIJING SQUARE

It was only a matter of time. For seven weeks the world had marveled at the restraint demonstrated by both Beijing's rulers and the thousands of demonstrators for democracy who had occupied Tiananmen Square. The whole affair, in fact, had developed the aura of a surrealistic ritual, with both sides' forces stepping in circles as if they were performing some stately, stylized pavane. Violence, it seemed, was out of the question. And then, early Sunday morning, the dance ended in a spasm of fury, the worst day of bloodshed in Communist China's history. **JUNE 12, 1989**

HIT: Comrades carry a *contra* wounded by a Sandinista sharpshooter out of action

SPACE

"OH, MY GOD!"

"Where in hell is the bird? Where is the bird?" shouted a space engineer at Cape Canaveral. "Oh, my God!" cried a teacher from the viewing stands nearby. "Don't let happen what I think just happened." Nancy Reagan, watching television in the White House family quarters, gasped similar words, "Oh, my God, no!" So too did William Graham, the acting administrator of NASA, who was watching in the office of a Congressman. "Oh, my God," he said. "Oh, my God." In one fiery instant, the nation's complacent attitude toward manned space flight had evaporated.   **FEB. 10, 1986**

MEDICINE

THE REAL EPIDEMIC: FEAR AND DESPAIR

In Manhattan last week a WABC-TV crew refused to enter the Gay Men's Health Crisis office to cover a story on AIDS. Two back-up crews also balked at going in. Said one of the technicians: "Look, nobody knows anything about AIDS. What makes them so cocksure I'm not going to get it from a sweaty palm?" One of the homosexuals in the office had a question of his own: "Do you understand now that we're treated like lepers?" As the deaths from AIDS-related diseases continue to rise, so does hysteria about possible contagion. AIDS victims and members of high-risk groups—male homosexuals, Haitians, hemophiliacs and intravenous drug users—are being shunned by their communities, even by their families.   **JULY 4, 1983**

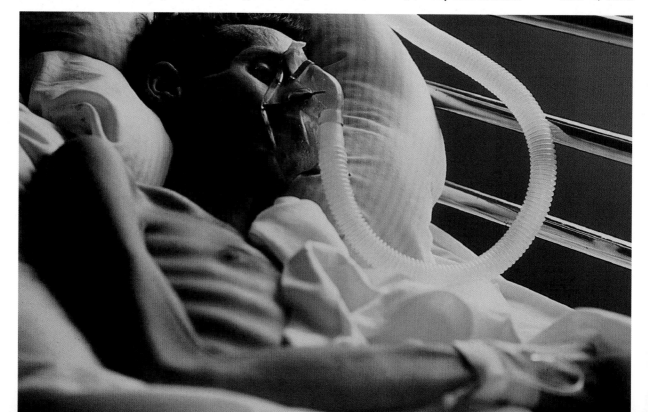

ENVIRONMENT

THE BIG BLOWUP

"Vancouver, Vancouver, this is it!" The frantic warning was radioed at precisely 8:31 a.m. on that fateful Sunday by Volcano Expert David Johnston, 30, who had climbed to a monitoring site five miles from Washington State's Mount St. Helens in the snow-capped Cascade Range, 40 miles northeast of Portland, Ore. ...

[Its] crater had been rumbling and steaming for eight weeks.

Seconds after his shouted message, a stupendous explosion of trapped gases, generating about 500 times the force of the atom bomb dropped on Hiroshima, blew the entire top off Mount St. Helens. In a single burst St. Helens was transformed from a postcard-symmetrical cone 9,667 ft. high to an ugly flat-top 1,300 ft. lower. Clouds of hot ash made up of pulverized rock were belched twelve miles into the sky.   **JUNE 2, 1980**

MEMORIALS

A HOMECOMING AT LAST

They came like pilgrims, bigger crowds each day, to Washington's newest and most unorthodox monument: the Viet Nam Veterans Memorial. Its long walls, inscribed with the names of 57,939 killed or missing in America's last war, are simple, elegant and dignified, everything the Viet Nam War was not. By the end of last week the adjacent ground was a fringe of private memorial icons: messages, photographs, candles and flags. **NOV. 22, 1982**

ENVIRONMENT

NIGHT OF DEATH

For almost an hour, the gas formed a vast, dense fog of death that drifted toward Bhopal. Through temples and shops, over streets and lakes, across a 25-sq.-mi. quadrant of the city, the cloud spread, noiselessly and lethally ... By week's end, 2,500 were dead. **DEC. 17, 1984**

WASTED: Colombian policemen dump confiscated cocaine

LIVING

REIGN OF COCAINE

Today, in part precisely because it is such an emblem of wealth and status, coke is the drug of choice for perhaps millions of solid, conventional and often upwardly mobile citizens. There is little likelihood that the cocaine blizzard will soon abate. A drug habit born of a desire to escape the bad news in life is not likely to be discouraged by the bad news about the drug itself. And so middle-class Americans continue to succumb to the powder's crystalline dazzle. Few are yet aware or willing to concede that at the least, taking cocaine is dangerous to their psychological health. It may be no easy task to re-convince them that good times are made, not sniffed. **MARCH 13, 1983**

MAN OF THE YEAR 1980–1988

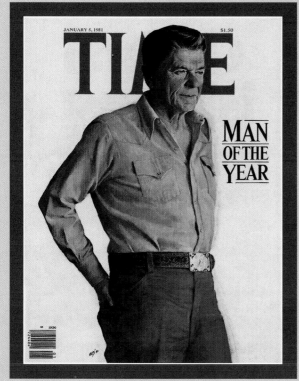

1980 After 20 years in which the White House was held by liberal Democrats John Kennedy and Lyndon Johnson and G.O.P. centrists Richard Nixon and Gerald Ford, Americans turned to the right in electing conservative **Ronald Reagan.**

1981 Solidarity leader **Lech Walesa** struck the first blows against the Kremlin's empire.

1982 Anticipating a revolution, TIME chose a Machine of the Year: **The Personal Computer.**

1983 Deadlocked: **Reagan and Andropov** failed to de-escalate the cold war missile race.

1984 Peter Ueberroth married Big Business to the Olympics with the profitable L.A. Games.

1985 Deng Xiaoping reshaped China, ditching Mao's leftist ideals for free-market reforms.

1986 Corazon Aquino led a peaceful revolution that ended the Marcos years in the Philippines.

1987 Unleashing *glasnost* and *perestroika,* **Mikhail Gorbachev** shattered Soviet lethargy.

1988 Eighteen years after the first Earth Day, TIME jump-started a new era of environmental activism with its surprise choice of **Endangered Earth** as Planet of the Year. The cover, a wrapped globe, was created by the contextual artist Christo.

PAINTING

THE POP SHOP

Pop strands are converging, it seems, at an accelerating rate. MTV has invented a genre and become an enormous success. Michael Jackson makes TV commercials for Pepsi. And the wall between pop and high culture that became a see-through membrane in the '60s and '70s today seems to be disintegrating ... Like Kurt Vonnegut's novels, Artist Keith Haring's doodly paintings are very very easy to like. In Manhattan, Haring just opened his own boutique, where he sells Haring buttons, watches, shirts and posters. It is called the Pop shop. **JUNE 16, 1986**

MUSIC

WHY SHE'S HOT

Now, then, parents, the important thing is to stay calm. You've seen Madonna wiggling on MTV—right, she's the pop-tart singer with the trashy outfits and the hi-there belly button. What is worse, your children have seen her. You tell your daughters to put on jeans and sweatshirts, like decent girls, and they look at you as if you've just blown in from the Planet of the Creeps. **MAY 27, 1985**

STEVE'S SUMMER MAGIC

E.T. is a miracle movie, and one that confirms Steven Spielberg as a master storyteller of his medium. Not since the glory days of Walt Disney Productions, when *Fantasia* and *Pinocchio* and *Dumbo* first worked their seductive magic, has a film so acutely evoked the twin senses of everyday wonder and otherworldly awe. **MAY 31, 1982**

THEATER

MEOW!

Cats is a musical that sweeps you off your feet but not into its arms. It is a triumph of motion over emotion, of EQ (energy quotient) over IQ. In *Cats*, the spectacle is the subject ... At the opening party the first reviews were more mixed than the drinks. **OCT. 18, 1982**

MUSIC

THRILLER

Michael Jackson may dance like Baryshnikov straddling a jackhammer, move like a street blood steeped in Astaire and t'ai chi, sing like an angel on a soul-food bender, but a fair portion of his personal taste and his musical inspiration comes from the sort of glitzy places where soul seldom strays. One of his favorite things is *My Favorite Things*, sung by Julie Andrews, raindrops on roses, warm woolen mittens and all. He loves the Beatles, and he also loves Gordon MacRae booming his way through *Oh What a Beautiful Morning*. He cares so little about conventional standards of hipness that he can rise above embarrassment on such matters. His catholicity directs him straight to the vital center of contemporary pop culture. **MARCH 19, 1984**

THE LAST DAY IN THE LIFE

Not just for his wife or son but for more people than anyone could ever begin to number, the killing of **John Lennon** was a death in the family ... His murder was an assassination, a ritual slaying of something that could hardly be named. Hope, perhaps; or idealism. **DEC. 22, 1980**

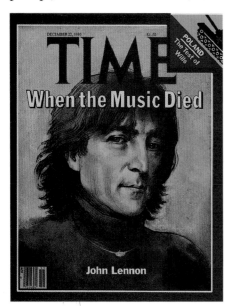

ON THEIR WAY

Breastplates glistened and the flanks of superbly groomed horses shone in the morning sunlight. Guardsmen's jackets seemed redder than they had any right to be. St. Paul's Cathedral tapered up into the sky like an exaltation in stone. Under the vaulting dome, **Charles and Diana** exchanged a whisper. **AUG. 10, 1981**

A BUMP, A SPIKE, A FALL

Mary Decker screamed and toppled forward. She landed hard on her left hip as she crashed in the grass infield. She tried to rise but could not. "I felt I was tied to the ground, and all I could do was watch them run off." **AUG. 20, 1984**

MONKEY BUSINESS

Gary Hart challenged the moralistic conventions of political behavior and ultimately paid the price for his apostasy. Until the very end Hart seemed oblivious to the reality that his actions had consequences. **MAY 18, 1987**

THE "IRON LADY" ON MANEUVERS

Prime Minister **Margaret Thatcher** was taking no flak last week as she fired a round from a Challenger tank at the NATO training ground near Fallingbostel, West Germany. Decked out in stout walking shoes, flowing scarf and goggles, Thatcher looked like "a cross between Isadora Duncan and Lawrence of Arabia," as the *Daily Telegraph* affectionately put it. With the help of a few tips from the Royal Hussars, the British leader sent a practice shell 1,000 yds. directly to its mark. "I loved it!" exclaimed the woman admirers and critics alike have dubbed the "Iron Lady." **SEPT. 29, 1986**

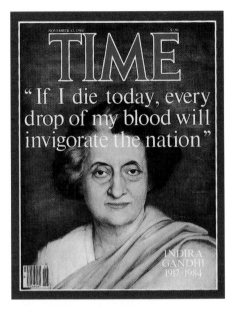

DEATH IN THE GARDEN

It was typical of the proud, stubborn, courageous **Indira Gandhi** that she hated to wear a bulletproof vest. The night before her death she told a large crowd: "I am not interested in a long life." **NOV. 12, 1984**

COSMIC ROVER, TODDLIN' TOWN

Physicist **Stephen Hawking** accompanied a group to a Chicago discotheque, where he joined in the festivities by wheeling onto the dance floor and spinning his chair in circles. Later, in a restaurant, a waiter passed the cork from a newly opened bottle of wine under Stephen's nose. The computer beeped, and the synthesized voice proclaimed, "Very good." **FEB. 8, 1988**

BORN-AGAIN DISASTER

On camera televangelist **Jim Bakker** displayed a disarming innocence that most viewers found appealing ... But off camera he was intensely shy and insecure, a melancholy man who once melted down his new wedding ring in a fit of jealousy over wife **Tammy Faye's** flirtation with Country Singer Gary Paxton and presented it to her as a pendant. **AUG. 3, 1987**

IMAGES
Photojournalism in TIME

CATCH! In November 1990, at a peak moment of his presidency, George Bush flings souvenir tie clips to U.S. troops in Saudi Arabia

D ue to technical demands, photographs in the early years of TIME were often limited to head shots of newsmakers: for decades the magazine's brisk words trumped its routine images. But beginning in the 1960s, and increasingly through the '70s, '80s and '90s, TIME became a showcase for gifted photojournalists, including the six individuals whose work is featured here.

DIANA WALKER

Great photojournalism relies on access to historic events and people, and TIME photographers fall into two general camps: passport-toting "outsiders," who travel to the front lines of the world's hot spots to capture images of war and revolution, and discreet "insiders," who gain access to tightly closed circles to catch privileged portraits of newsmakers in action. Two of the most distinguished of the latter group are TIME political photographers Diana Walker and P.F. Bentley.

Walker's photographs first appeared in TIME in 1976; she has been assigned to the White House for the magazine since 1984. In 1989 her photoessay "A Day in the Life of George Bush" was a major exclusive for TIME; her 1990 picture of the President gracefully tossing White House souvenirs to American troops stationed in Saudi Arabia before the Gulf War, left, was awarded the first prize in the World Press Photo competition. Her behind-the-scenes images for TIME of Bill Clinton's re-election campaign in 1996 also received numerous awards.

WHAT'S SO FUNNY? A royal jest about the weather earns a presidential laugh, 1983

P.F. BENTLEY

"P.F.'s passion is recording history as it happens," says TIME picture editor Michele Stephenson. "He has great instincts, and he gets rare access because his subjects trust him." His secret: never getting in the way, and never revealing what he hears. Bentley has photographed every major presidential contender since 1980, and he has parlayed his unique, fly-on-the-wall view of the private moments of Washington's élite into a remarkable portrait gallery of American political life at the close of the century. He has published two books based on his work for TIME, *Clinton: Portrait of Victory* (1993), and *Newt: Inside the Revolution* (1995).

FAREWELL: Bob Dole weeps at a private gathering of Senators who toasted his decision to leave the Hill in 1996. Bentley knew of Dole's surprise in advance

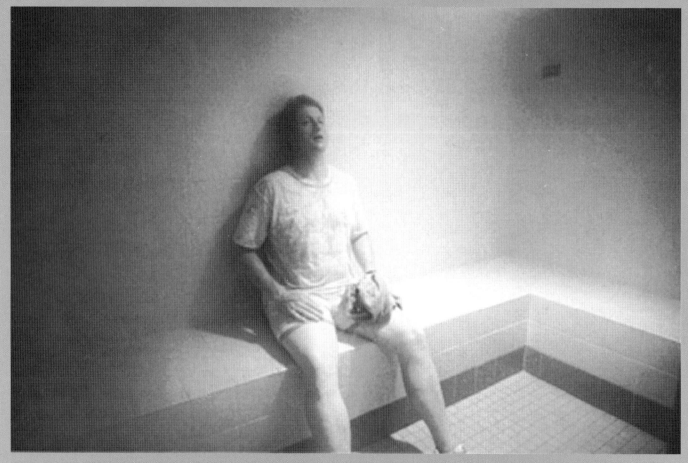

WHIPPED: Bill Clinton moisturizes his ragged vocal cords in a steam room before accepting his party's nomination, July 1992

THE END: Family and friends at the coffin of Chicago's Robert ("Yummy") Sandifer, 11, killed by members of his own gang in Chicago

STEVE LISS

Like Diana Walker and P.F. Bentley, Steve Liss is a veteran political photographer: his 1970s photos of busing oppo-nents chasing Senator Ted Kennedy down a Massachusetts street were among his first award winners. But Liss is also a master photographer of everyday life; he says his favorite assignments are long-term mood pieces of rural Americans, like his 1991 TIME pictures of the lives of the poor in the Mississippi Delta. As the photos on this page attest, Liss's great strength is his remarkable ability to document the lives of people who normally would not be consid-ered newsmakers, by gaining access to their most private moments.

DOWN AND OUT: In 1995 Liss photographed Robert Givens and son Rory at home, a motel room that housed Givens' wife, six kids, 11 cats, two lizards and a puppy

REMEMBRANCE: Swathed head to foot in the traditional burkah, a woman in Afghanistan mourns a brother lost in the civil war, 1996

JAMES NACHTWEY

Each year the Overseas Press Club awards the prestigious Robert Capa Gold Medal to the photographer whose pictures best live up to the great standard of foreign news photography established by Capa, the legendary cameraman whose images of the Spanish Civil War and World War II are among the most memorable in the history of photojournalism. Capa, who died on assignment in Indochina in 1954, once said, "If your pictures aren't good enough, you're not close enough."

TIME photographer James Nachtwey gets "close enough"—and he has four Capa medals to prove it. In his 17 years of pho-tographing conflict around the world, Nachtwey has repeatedly put himself in danger to get an image. On assignment for TIME in South Africa a week before the historic April 1994 elections, Nachtwey was with a group of photographers near Johannesburg when government troops opened fire on them. As photographer Greg Marinovich fell to the ground, wounded, Nachtwey began pulling him to safety. Then he noticed that another colleague, Ken Oosterbroek, had also been hit. "I laid Greg down, told him I'd be back, and as I was crawling to Ken, one of the soldiers fired," Nachtwey recalls. As he scrambled across the street, a bullet passed so close to his head that it literally parted his hair. When he reached his friend, Oosterbroek was dead.

HOME: This boy survived the battles that destroyed Grozny, Chechnya, 1996. His parents did not

STARVATION: A famine victim in Sudan crawls past a relief hut, 1993. Readers often inquire if such grim images must run, but TIME's editors argue they reflect reality, however appalling to behold

GRIEF: A Croatian youngster cries at the funeral of his father, a policeman killed in a clash with Serbs in September 1991

CHRISTOPHER MORRIS

A 1990s version of the great combat photographers of World War II, Christopher Morris has worn out his passport chronicling the world's danger zones. He has shot revolutions in the Philippines and Chechnya, the wars of Colombian drug lords, guerrilla strife in Afghanistan, the U.S. invasion of Panama and the fall of the Berlin Wall. Shooting the Gulf War in 1991, he was captured by Iraqi troops and held in Baghdad. In Sarajevo in 1995 the skin of his armored pickup was pierced by bullets while Morris was outside the truck, pinned down by snipers for two hours before French peace-keeping troops rescued him.

ON THE RUN: A trapped Chechen soldier dashes headlong into Russian fire, 1995. Morris calls this one of the most dangerous combat situations he has ever shot

ANTHONY SUAU

Civil war in Ethiopia. Revolt in the former Soviet Union. The Gulf War. The plight of the Kurds. The funeral of Ayatullah Khomeini: Anthony Suau has photographed these historic events and many more. Small wonder the subject closest to his heart is a personal project he calls "Gentler Moments," a study of the humble people of the Romanian countryside. For a 1991 TIME cover story, Suau retraced a trip made 60 years before by photojournalist Margaret Bourke-White and returned with memorable images of life in today's Russia, including the picture at right.

IRON AGE: A steel mill in the Ural Mountains, from Suau's 1991 TIME cover story

EARLY DEATH: The morning wears a shroud of mist in Suau's 1991 picture of the burial of a Kurdish child at a refugee camp in Turkey

1989-1998

TRANSFORM

INFO OVERLOAD
**Before it could even be realized,
the dream of 500 video channels
morphed into millions of Websites**

ATION

As the cold war recedes into history, American ideals, American capitalism and American technology have emerged as the world's engine of change

Michael Kinsley

TECHNOLOGY, DEMOCRACY, MONEY

History is not over. In fact, there's more of it than ever

A SOVIETOLOGIST NAMED FRANCIS FUKUYAMA PUBLISHED A PROVOCATIVE ESSAY called "The End of History?" in the waning months of the 1980s. Fukuyama's thesis—that the collapse of the Soviet Union meant people would have nothing more to fight wars about—was soon disproved. The 1990s have not been short on history. The end of the cold war defrosted earlier rivalries that had been frozen for two generations, bringing bloody history back to places like Bosnia, where it had been in cold storage. The 1990s, however, have indeed been a period when the great arguments about how society should be organized seemed settled. Democracy blossomed in South Africa and Russia; even Vietnam embraced capitalism.

Nevertheless, life has not been boring. If the melodrama of history has been

subdued, the melodrama of technology burns bright. We still live in interesting times. Is it the blinkered arrogance of the present to think of the 1990s as the decade of technology? Every decade in the 75 years since TIME was founded has seen everyday life transformed by invention. Is the Internet more life-transforming than household electricity? Or air travel? Or television, frozen food and microwave ovens (to defrost the frozen food)? Maybe technology isn't changing our lives faster than ever, but it certainly seems that way. Did Clarence Birdseye become the richest man in the world? Appear four times on TIME's cover? Did he become, as Bill Gates has, a cultural icon, right up there with the beautiful princess who died with her lover in a car crash in Paris?

Technology, democracy and capitalism, the themes of this decade, interreact. PCs may have been born in the '80s, but the productivity payoff came in the '90s. (It took 10 years to figure out how to use the damned things!) Thus technology added mightily to this decade's prosperity, which reinforced the prestige of capitalism. Capitalism, meanwhile, repaid the favor. A few years ago, there was talk of the government's spending billions to build the "information superhighway." Then that highway sprang up overnight. The Web's sudden arrival as a society-transforming force is largely the result of capitalism in almost textbook-pure form: not IBM or even Microsoft, but vast crowds of garage-shop inventors and hungry entrepreneurs.

TECHNOLOGY ALSO PROMOTES DEMOCRACY—the exact opposite of what Orwell foresaw. The fax machine helped bring down communism, and the Net makes state control of information impossible. Even in free countries, citizens have new powers to communicate with and about their elected rulers. A.J. Liebling said that freedom of the press was guaranteed only to those who own one. Now almost anyone can.

History is not over; in fact, there's more of it than ever before. It depends on written records, and the thrust of communications technology has been to make those records richer and more finely grained. The telephone, in that respect, was a step backward; it encouraged decision making without keeping a contemporaneous record. Now, between E-mail and camcorders, we may have more history than we know what to do with. ∎

GRIEF: A sergeant hears that a body bag, above, holds a friend

THE BATTLEGROUND
100 HOURS

General Norman Schwarzkopf seemed right in terming the coalition's ability to achieve nearly total success with so few losses "almost miraculous." Not only were the pessimists and skeptics wrong ... but the optimists were far off the mark too. American casualties were less than 5% of the *lowest* prewar Pentagon estimates. U.S. forces had prepared about 10,000 beds, aboard ships and in three field hospitals, to receive the wounded; only a tiny fraction were filled. Such overwhelming success, in fact, may be unrepeatable. **MARCH 11, 1991**

A FIRST THICK SHOCK OF WAR

The coming of war brought a scrapbook of gestures, like snapshots tucked into history. It was a week of yellow ribbons, blood donations, hastily drawn wills. Two frat boys at Oklahoma State kept vigil in a tree house to support the troops in the gulf. A disabled Vietnam veteran paid the Arkansas Flag & Banner Co. $45 to make him an Iraqi flag so that he could burn it. In Boulder, Army Reservist Christopher Minney married his sweetheart Melonie Walter on Wednesday, as soon as he heard that he would have to report for duty the following day

The first thick shock of war brought more hymns than marches, as though the nation had matured enough to know that battle isn't the way it looks in the movies—or even in the strangely antiseptic images of the air war flickering across television screens. Among those Americans who supported the President's actions—a solid majority, according to most polls—there was little gloating or shiny jingoism.   **JAN. 28, 1991**

KUWAIT

SADDAM'S PARTING SHOT

No one will have much oil to refine until fire fighters extinguish the Iraqi-set blazes that raged last week through more than 500 of Kuwait's 1,000 wells, blackening the country's sky. It will require millions of gallons of water and tons of dynamite to snuff out the flames. "It's one gigantic mess," says Red Adair, whose Houston company is one of four Texas firms engaged in the effort. "No one knows what we're really in for. I've never seen anything like this in my life."   **MARCH 11, 1991**

GULF WAR

LIBERATING KUWAIT

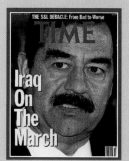

1990 In August Iraq's **Saddam Hussein,** "a blood-drenched tyrant," invaded Kuwait for oil.

1991 Prime-time war: CNN brought the allies' **Bombing of Baghdad** into the living room.

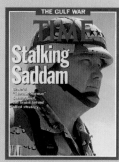

1991 General Norman Schwarzkopf: "ambition … abiding certitude … bristling self-assurance."

1991 Only 100 hours after invading occupied Kuwait, U.S. troops celebrated their **Victory.**

CULTS

APOCALYPSE NOW

David Koresh—high school dropout, rock musician, polygamist, preacher—built his church on a simple message: "If the Bible is true, then I'm Christ." It was enough to draw more than a hundred people to join him at an armed fortress near Waco, Texas … The same message tempted Koresh to entertain a vision of martyrdom for himself. He would die in a battle against unbelievers, then be joined in heaven by the followers who chose to lay down their lives for him. On April 19 a gigantic fireball consumed the compound Koresh had named Ranch Apocalypse, and his vision was granted.   **MAY 3, 1993**

JUSTICE

IF IT DOESN'T FIT …

As the prosecution team slowly moved to its conclusion, it committed its greatest blunder. Christopher Darden, Marcia Clark's second-in-command, had been told by his supervisors not to make a show of the gloves. But impetuously he asked Simpson to try them on. The defense had anticipated the move and had coached Simpson's response. Simpson at first struggled to pull on the supposedly incriminating gloves, then turned toward the jury, raised his half-gloved hands and proclaimed dramatically, "They're too small." Darden quickly suggested that Simpson was faking his difficulty, then solicited expert testimony that the blood-soaked leather gloves had shrunk. But the damage had been done.   **JUNE 26, 1995**

TERRORISM

THE BLOOD OF INNOCENTS

How much practice did it take to plan a human sacrifice? … When the day finally came, the truck loaded and the time set, did the killers wait and watch the children go in, hand in hand, with their parents, before they drove away?

The whole world watched the children come out. The lucky ones sobbed and bled and called brokenly for the parents they had left only minutes before. Most of their friends remained buried inside. The rescuers wept as they cradled them, limp and weightless; fire fighters could not bear to look down at the children in their arms. "Find out who did this," one told Oklahoma Governor Frank Keating. "All that I have found are a baby's finger and an American flag."   **MAY 1, 1995**

PHOTO-OP STOP

In September, White House photographer Barbara Kinney caught a covey of world leaders as they prepared for the signing of the historic accord expanding Palestinian self-rule. Reports Kinney: "An aide said, 'Oh, Mr. Clinton, your tie's a bit crooked. You might want to fix that.' He did, and out of the corner of my eye, I realized they were all doing it out of instinct." [Picture and text from TIME's annual Images section of the year's most memorable photographs.] **DEC. 25, 1995**

SOUTH AFRICA

FREE AT LAST

At 4:15 p.m. local time on Sunday, Feb. 11, Nelson Mandela walked out of the Victor Verster Prison Farm near Cape Town—free at last. It was, said the official South African Broadcasting Corp., "the moment that a majority of South Africans, and the world, have been waiting for." A bulky 200-pounder when the doors closed behind him, Mandela is now a slim, white-haired statesman of 71. He referred to his quarter-century behind bars as "long, lonely, wasted years." **FEB. 19, 1990**

RUSSIA

RED OCTOBER

On Sunday, Oct. 3, a gang of hard-liners, fascists, communists and nationalists rampaged 10,000-strong through the streets of Moscow, braving a hail of rubber bullets and tear gas from troops loyal to Yeltsin. Breaching police lines, the demonstrators recaptured the plaza behind the barricaded White House. Then, after a fiery address from Vice President Alexander Rutskoi [the Afghan war hero who had been Yeltsin's ally during the failed coup attempt in August 1991], commanding them to "stand up, take positions ... and attack," they grabbed shields and guns from their opponents, commandeered military vehicles and seized control of Ostenkino, the national television broadcasting center. **OCT. 11, 1993**

MAN OF THE YEAR 1990-1998

1990 TIME named **Mikhail Gorbachev** "Man of the Decade" for his revolutionary policies.

1992 With CNN's broadcasts from Moscow and Baghdad, **Ted Turner** revolutionized the news.

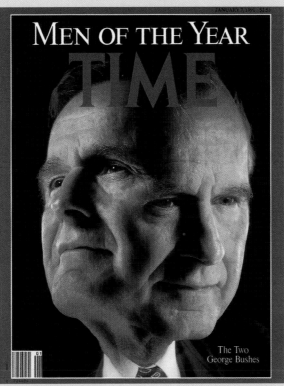

1991 Leading an allied coalition that stood up to Iraqi strongman Saddam Hussein, George Bush was decisive. Facing a feeble economy at home, he waffled. Gregory Heisler's striking photograph caught both sides of **The Two George Bushes.**

1993 Ending a 12-year G.O.P. run, **Bill Clinton** brought Democrats back to the White House.

1994 Arafat and Rabin, Mandela and De Klerk made 1994 the year of **The Peacemakers.**

1997 "For helping lift a death sentence—for a few years at least, and perhaps longer—on tens of thousands of AIDS sufferers, and for pioneering the treatment that might, just might, lead to a cure, **David Da-i Ho, M.D.,** is TIME's Man of the Year."

1995 Even in his 70s, **Pope John Paul II** traveled widely to express his conservative views.

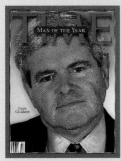

1996 Newt Gingrich spearheaded the G.O.P.'s sweeping—and historic—congressional victory.

1998 Andy Grove: the tough boss of giant chipmaker Intel helped lead the digital revolution.

BIOLOGY

THE AGE OF CLONING

Researchers at the Roslin Institute near Edinburgh, Scotland, pulled off what many experts thought might be a scientific impossibility. From a cell in an adult ewe's mammary gland, embryologist Ian Wilmut and his colleagues managed to create a frisky lamb named Dolly (with apologies to Ms. Parton), scoring an advance in reproductive technology as unsettling as it was startling. Unlike offspring produced in the usual fashion, Dolly does not merely take after her biological mother: she is a carbon copy, a laboratory counterfeit so exact that she is in essence her mother's identical twin. **MARCH 10, 1997**

SPACE

RETURN TO MARS

There was no one in Mars' Ares Vallis floodplain to mark the moment when NASA's 3-ft.-tall Pathfinder spacecraft dropped into the soil of the long-dry valley. But there was a planet more than 100 million miles away filled with people who were paying heed when it landed, appropriately enough, on July 4. For the first time in 21 years, a machine shot from Earth once again stirred up the Martian dust. More important, for the first time ever, it was going to be able to keep stirring it up well after it landed. Curled up inside Pathfinder like a mechanical kangaroo joey was Sojourner, a 1-ft.-tall, 2-ft.-long robot car, known as a rover, designed to trundle away from the lander and investigate rocks all over the desert-like site. **JULY 14, 1997**

1994 A year later, **the Internet** was "a working prototype of the Information Superhighway."

1996 Golden Geeks like Netscape's Marc Andreessen staked claims on the World Wide Web.

1997 Steve Case of America Online helped turn cyberspace into a mainstream medium.

SPACE

COSMIC CLOSE-UPS

They look remarkably like great towering thunderheads, billowing high into the evening sky as they catch the last rays of the setting sun. These are no ordinary clouds, however. They stand not 30,000 ft. but almost 6 trillion miles high. They are illuminated not with ordinary earthly light but with searing ultraviolet radiation spewing from nuclear fires at the center of a handful of newly formed stars. And they're 7,000 light-years from Earth—more than 400 million times as far away as the sun. This cosmic vista is the latest in a series of stunning images captured from the ends of the universe by the Hubble Space Telescope. Once written off as a near total loss because of an inaccurately ground mirror, the Hubble has in the past two years redeemed itself spectacularly.   **NOV. 20, 1995**

DESIGN

BRAVO, BILBAO!

Frank Gehry's Guggenheim Museum has hit Bilbao, Spain, with the force of an architectural meteorite. No question that it's there. You're walking through the pleasantly undistinguished 19th century streets; you turn a corner, and—*pow!*—an apparition appears in glass and half-shiny silver (titanium, actually), massively undulating, something that seems to have been dropped from another world.

NOV. 3, 1997

MUSIC

DEATH OF A "GANGSTA"

Tupac Shakur became a gangsta rap star who sold more than 10 million albums. His life—and then his death—came to imitate his art. His songs were laced with sneers at "bitches" and the cop-killing taunts of gangstaism; he carried a gun and shot at people. He escaped conviction on a series of assault charges, but a 1993 sexual-abuse complaint stuck … He was cut down in a hail of bullets in Las Vegas. No arrests were made in the murder.   **SEPT. 23, 1996**

MUSIC

GURU OF GRUNGE

Nirvana's Kurt Cobain, dead at 27. The news came as a shock to millions of rock fans. Given Cobain's talent and influence as a songwriter and bandleader, the reaction was understandable. *Nevermind*, released in 1991 … fibrillated the psyche of a generation and launched the vogue for grunge.   **APRIL 18, 1994**

THEATER

GAY WHITE WAY

Angels in America galvanized audiences with its radical political perspective and literary style … [Tony Kushner's play] disproved truisms about the unmarketability of political drama with its aggressive scorn for Ronald Reagan and Republicanism, for Mormons and moralizing, and its demonic view of lawyer-dealmaker Roy Cohn, a gay-bashing closet gay and a top-level G.O.P. influence peddler for more than three decades. Instead, the play compellingly reasserted the theater's place in the public debate.   **DEC. 6, 1993**

CINEMA

SINKING FEELING

Tales of *Titanic*'s agonizing gestation and tardy birth … will mean little to moviegoers, who will pay the same $7 or $8 to see *Titanic* that they spend on films made for a thousandth its cost. *Titanic* will sail or sink not on its budget but on its merits as drama and spectacle. The verdict here: Dead in the water.   **DEC. 8, 1997**

SEEKER OF SOULS

Despite her celebrity, **Mother Teresa** had a faith that was not of this world. She was intent on saving souls in an era that no longer believed souls existed … She was not some saintly relic but a willing servant of her God: "I am like a little pencil in [God's] hand. He does the writing. The pencil exists only to be used."   SEPT. 15, 1997

DEATH OF A PRINCESS

Her public courtship with Dodi Fayed was a sign that **Princess Diana** was putting her past behind her. But it was only last week, in an interview with a French newspaper, that she made clear how completely she was cutting her emotional ties both to the life she had led and the press that had made it the trial it was. "Any sane person," she said forthrightly, "would have left [Britain] long ago."   **SEPT. 8, 1997**

TRACKING DOWN THE UNABOMBER

Sometimes **Ted Kaczynski** would stay inside for weeks at a stretch. You could smell him coming, steeped in woodsmoke … The dogs figured him out long before the feds did. "All the dogs hated him," recalled a longtime local.   **APRIL 15, 1996**

MR. NATURAL

To the medical establishment, his stories are the worst kind of hooey … but **Dr. Andrew Weil** is the man of the moment in America's eternal search for an alternative to conventional, interventionist, pharmaceutical medicine.   **MAY 12, 1997**

GREAT LEAPIN' LIZARDS!

For **Michael Jordan,** the world of basketball is a world without bounds. He gyrates, levitates and often dominates. Certainly he fascinates. In arenas around the country, food and drink go unsold because fans refuse to leave their seats for fear of missing a spectacular Jordan move to tell their grandchildren about. **JAN. 19, 1989**

VENDETTA ON ICE

Poor **Tonya Harding.** The would-be queen of figure skating was the bead of raw sweat in a field of dainty perspirers, the pool-playing, drag-racing, trash-talking bad girl in a sport that thrives on illusion. While rivals floated through their programs, she bullied gravity, fighting it off like a mugger. "To be perfectly honest," she said, "what I'm really thinking about is dollar signs." **JAN. 24, 1994**

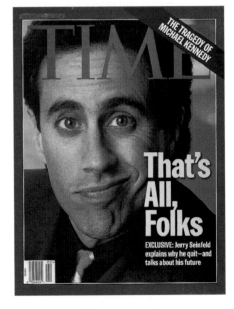

A QUESTION OF CHARACTER

If Clarence Thomas had been a woman, he might have been **Anita Hill.** The childhood without much money, the hard work that led to Yale Law School, the achievements in public service—much of Thomas' up-by-the-bootstraps life story has its equivalent in hers. And just as his reputation for integrity makes the charges against him hard to believe, her reputation makes them hard to dismiss. **OCT. 21, 1991**

FROM YADDA TO NADA

Jerry Seinfeld is in the curious position of facing, at a relatively tender age (43), a sort of retirement. He is the Bill Clinton of comedy, the boy wonder as lame duck—if only, that is, Seinfeld were more desperate to be loved. **JAN. 12, 1998**

Walter Isaacson

LUCE'S VALUES—THEN AND NOW

We still believe "the world is round" and embrace "an interest in the new"

WHEN HENRY LUCE AND BRITON HADDEN FOUNDED TIME 75 years ago, they felt that folks were being bombarded with information but were nevertheless woefully underinformed. They set out to create a magazine that would sift through the clutter, synthesize what was important and preach their cheeky prejudices.

We're now faced with a world that is far more saturated with information than they could have imagined: scores of TV networks, hundreds of magazines, thousands of electronic sources— all brimming with headlines and hype, news and sleaze, smart analysis and kooky opining.

What is the role of a general-interest newsmagazine in such an environment? Obviously, it's changed a lot in 75 years. We no longer offer a digest of last week's news, since we assume our readers are familiar with most of the headlines. Instead, we try to put events into context, anticipate trends, add new insights and facts, tell the behind-the-scene tales and explore the questions others forgot to ask.

But one aspect of our magazine's original mission has been, we believe, strengthened. The proliferation of magazines, channels and news services means that much of the media has become narrowly focused on special interests and niches. Yet we hold to the faith that intelligent people are curious about what's new in all sorts of fields, from politics to art, religion to technology. Just like us, they can be interested in both Saddam Hussein and Monica Lewinsky, Andrew Grove and Princess Diana, Toni Morrison and Jerry Seinfeld, Bill Clinton and Bill Gates.

So each week we have the joy of bringing together a mix of stories that conveys the excitement of our times in all its diversity. This mission helps us promote the rewards of serendipity, such as when a reader who is most interested in U.S. or world issues stumbles across something intriguing about medicine or music. It also helps us play a role that has become increasingly valuable in a world in which so many endeavors are hyperlinked: providing the common ground of information and knowledge that all informed folks should share and in fact

enjoy sharing, whatever their specialized interests may be.

We also offer, or at least try to, a philosophical common ground. Since the great left-right struggles of the 1960s through '80s, the world has entered a millennial period in which common sense plays a greater role than knee-jerk ideological faiths. Although our stories often have a strong point of view, we try to make sure they are informed by open-minded reporting rather than partisan biases.

Yes, that represents a change from the days when Luce's global agendas infused TIME's pages. The son of a Presbyterian missionary in China, Luce inherited a zeal to spread American values and Christianize the communist world. He was very upfront about his approach. In the prospectus that he wrote with Hadden, he noted that "complete neutrality ... is probably as undesirable as it is impossible," and he proceeded to lay out a litany of what would be the new magazine's "prejudices."

As TIME matured, it began to place more emphasis on reporting than on these prejudices. Nevertheless, there are certain prejudices— perhaps it's best to call them values—in the original prospectus that still inform TIME's journalism.

The foremost of these is the one Luce listed first: "A belief that the world is round." Luce was allergic to isolationism. In his famous 1941 essay, "The American Century," he urged the nation to engage in a global struggle on behalf of its values, most notably "a love of freedom, a feeling for the equality of opportunity, a tradition of self-reliance and independence and also of cooperation."

As the American Century draws to an end, these values are now ascendant. The main, albeit unfinished, story line of the century is the triumph of freedom (and its corollaries: democracy, individual liberty and free markets) over totalitarianism and communism. When America has been willing to stand firm for its values, that willingness has proved to be, even more than its military might, the true source of its power in the world. TIME thus remains rather prejudiced toward the values of free minds, free markets, free speech and free choice. This reflects our faith that people are generally smart and sensible; the more choices and information they have, the better off things will be. To the extent that America remains an avatar of freedom, the Global Century about to dawn will be another American Century.

In a world that is not only round but also wired and networked, we remain committed to another prejudice in the original prospectus: "an interest in the new." The digital revolution, in particular, has the potential to change our world like nothing else since the invention of television.

Because we believe in the value of information, we have celebrated the explosion of sources that is the hallmark of the digital age. It is not only healthy for the public, it is also healthy for us. In a world of a thousand voices, people will gravitate to those they trust. That encourages us to stick to a formula that is clear yet demanding: good reporting, good writing, authoritative and fair analysis. In addition, a continually refreshed diversity of sources helps counterbalance the trend (of which TIME and its parent, Time Warner, are a part) toward media conglomeration. We wouldn't be in this business if we didn't believe that more information and more opinions will eventually lead to more truth. That is why we were among the first journalists to go online and on the Web, and why we have pushed for open systems, like the Internet, that allow a diversity of voices to join the fray.

TIME's emphasis on narrative storytelling as a way to put events into context suits a weekly magazine. TV and the Internet are good for instant headlines and punditry. The Web is great for exploring links and drilling down for raw data. But TIME can play the storyteller who comes to your front porch with the color and insights that turn facts into coherent narratives. Part of the process is telling the news through the people who make it. As TIME's prospectus put it: "It is important to know what they drink. It is more important to know to what gods they pray and what kind of fights they love."

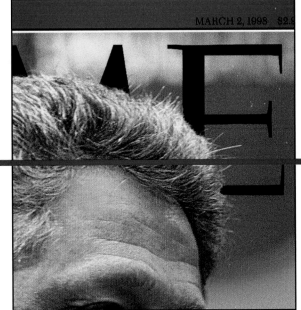

Through narrative and personality, analysis and synthesis, we try to make a complex world more coherent. The ultimate goal is to help make sure that the chaotic tumble of progress does not outpace our moral processing power. A classic example came the week that World War II ended. TIME's cover stories, led by the writing of the great James Agee, focused on the dropping of the atom bomb [*see text on page 70*]. Later in that issue, in a new section called Atomic Age, TIME wrestled with the historic and moral implications of what passed for progress:

> *Pain and a price attended progress. The last great convulsion brought steam and electricity, and with them an age of confusion and mounting war. A dim folk memory had preserved the story of a greater advance: "the winged hound of Zeus" tearing from Prometheus' liver the price of fire. Was the world ready for the new step forward? It was never ready. It was, in fact, still fumbling for the answers to the age of steam and electricity. Man had been tossed into the vestibule of another millennium. It was wonderful to think of what the Atomic Age might be, if man was strong and honest. But at first it was a strange place, full of weird symbols and the smell of death.*

THE VESTIBULE OF THIS NEW MILLENNIUM STILL HAS INTRUDERS that TIME tries to wrestle into moral and historical context. The digital age has brought not only the excitement of more democratic forms of media but also the specter of invasions of our privacy and the spread of false information and poisonous ideas to every nook of a networked world. The impending biotech age promises not only the ability to engineer an end to diseases but also the weird prospects of cloning our bodies and tinkering with the genes of our children.

Nevertheless, the prejudice that we most firmly share with Luce and Hadden is a fundamental optimism. For them, optimism—a faith in progress—was not just a creed, it was a tactic for making things better. The challenges of a new millennium as well as today's fin-de-siècle scandals require that reporters be skeptical. But we must avoid the journalistic cynicism—as a pose, a sophomoric attitude—that reigned in the '70s and '80s. Intelligent skepticism can, and should, be compatible with a basic belief in progress and a faith in humanity's capacity for common sense.

Our goal is to be a touchstone for this common sense. Rather than strike a pose of pessimism about all values, we must hew to certain basic ones, such as doing what's best for our kids. Rather than view individual rights as being at odds with a compassionate sense of community, we must understand that America's historic magic has been to create a social fabric that is strong because it weaves these two strands together.

"As a journalist," Luce once said, "I am in command of a small sector in the very front trenches of this battle for freedom." Above all, we continue to share his belief that journalism can be, at its best, a noble endeavor. It can make people think—and make them think differently. It can be empowering and liberating. And, of course, it can be fun and exciting. That's what Luce sought to impart in his new magazine, and what we seek to impart in our new one each week. ∎

WALTER ISAACSON *is the 14th managing editor of* TIME *magazine. A former editor of new media for Time Inc., he is the author of* Kissinger: A Biography.

INDEX

INDEX

CREDITS

Credits read from left to right and from top to bottom of page, except as noted. All TIME covers © Time Inc.

FRONT COVER UPI/Corbis-Bettmann, Photoworld/FPG, UPI/Corbis-Bettmann, Vernon Merritt/LIFE, Michael Evans/Gamma Liaison

CONTENTS iv Hulton Getty/Tony Stone Images, G.A. Douglas/R.I. Nesmith & Associates, UPI/Corbis Bettmann, J.R. Eyerman/LIFE **v** David Gahr, Alain Mingam/Gamma Liaison, Anthony Suau/Gamma Liaison, © Louis Psyhosis/Matrix

LETTERS 2 Globe Photos, UPI/Corbis-Bettmann **3** Peter Stackpole/LIFE, George Karger/LIFE, Globe Photos, Courtesy William F. Buckley, Hans Wild/LIFE, Photofest **4** AP/Wide World, Murray Garrett/Graphic House/Archive, Howell Conant/LIFE, Orion Press, Camera Press/Retna, no credit **5** Michael Renard, Robert L. Miller, UPI/Corbis-Bettmann, Vernon Merritt/LIFE, Photofest, AP/Wide World **6** no credit, Donald Sanders/Globe Photos, Michael Evans/Gamma Liaison, David Hume Kennerly, Thomas Victor, Nate Cutler/Globe Photos **7** Diana Walker, Michael Mauney, Topham/The Image Works, Fitzroy Barrett/Retna, Photofest, Celebrity Photo

A HISTORY/A LIFE 8 Time Inc. Archives **9** U.S. Marine Corps Photo, Time Inc. Archives **10** R.R. Donnelley & Sons Archives, no credit **11** Terry Smith, Robert Maass **12** Burt Glinn/Magnum **13** Time Inc. Archives (4)

NOTEBOOK 14 (clockwise from Luce) M. Norton/Time Archives, Sonia Moskowitz, Robert Maass, Diana Walker, Time Archives, Margaret Bourke-White for TIME, no credit **15** (clockwise from Moore) Robert Maass, Doug Goodman, Sonia Moskowitz, Patrick McMullen, Diana Walker, no credit (2), Paul Thompson/FPG, **16** (clockwise from Sinatra) Sam Shaw, Carl Mydans/LIFE (2), no credit **17** (clockwise from Monk) Paul J. Joeffler/Frank Driggs Collection, Lynn Pelham, Tom Arma, no credit (2), UPI/Corbis-Bettmann **16-17** (cartoons, left to right) Everett Opie©1958, Richard McCallister©1979, Dana Fradon ©1959, Everett Opie©1988—all © from *The New Yorker* Collection. All rights reserved. **18** no credits **19** Courtesy the *Harvard Lampoon* (3) **14-19** (illustrations) Matthew Martin

EXUBERANCE 20 Hulton Getty/Tony Stone Images **21** UPI/Corbis-Bettmann **22-23** Culver Pictures, Frank Driggs Collection, Peter Mauss/Esto Photographics, ©Walt Disney Inc., Oscar White/Corbis **24** UPI/Corbis-Bettmann (2) **25** Culver Pictures, no credit **26** UPI/Corbis-Bettmann, no credit, National Archives **27** ©Vithalbhai Collection/DPA/The Image Works, no credit **28** UPI/Corbis-Bettmann, Mansell/Time Inc. **29** Underwood & Underwood **30** Corbis-Bettmann, Library of Congress/Corbis **31** no credit, Photofest, Maurice Beck & Macgregor **32** Wide World, no credit, Keystone View **33** ©Time Inc., UPI/Corbis-Bettmann, no credit

DESPAIR 34 Mario Fenyo **35** G.A. Douglas/R.I. Nesmith & Associates **36-37** Arthur Rothstein/Library of Congress, UPI/Corbis-Bettmann, Photoworld/FPG,

Brown Brothers **38** Wide World, Tennessee Valley Authority **39** AP/Wide World, no credit **40** UPI/Corbis-Bettmann **41** Wide World, UPI/Corbis-Bettmann **42** AP/Wide World, UPI/Corbis-Bettmann **44** Alfred Eisenstaedt/LIFE, Vandamm Studio, Photofest **45** Vandamm Studio, Photofest **46** James Jarche/Popperfoto, Rev. F.D. Learner & George Fitch, UPI/Corbis-Bettmann **47** UPI/Corbis-Bettmann, Wide World, Underwood & Underwood

PORTRAITS 49 Eric Schaal/LIFE **50** Erika **51** Walter Daran **53** Susan Biddle/The White House

WAR 56-57 UPI/Corbis-Bettmann **58-59** Gjon Mili/LIFE, UPI/Corbis-Bettmann, Culver Pictures, Alfred Eisenstaedt/LIFE, U.S. Army **60** Julien Bryan/Robert Hunt Library, United Israel Appeal **61** UPI/Corbis-Bettmann **62** UPI/Corbis-Bettmann **63** U.S. Army/AP/Wide World, Robert Capa/Magnum **64** Yevgeny Khaldei, U.S. Army Air Forces, U.S. Signal Corps **66-67** U.S. Navy **68** Carl Mydans/LIFE, Defense Department Photo **69** U.S. Coast Guard/UPI/Corbis-Bettmann, Carl Mydans/LIFE **70-71** Bernard Hoffman/LIFE **72** Nat Fein/AP/Wide World, Photoworld/FPG, UPI/Corbis-Bettmann, Wide World **73** UPI/Corbis-Bettmann, Wide World, AP/Wide World, Wallace Kirkland/LIFE

AFFLUENCE 74 Joe Scherschel/LIFE **75** Ed Bailey **76-77** W. Wolff, John Bryson©Time Inc., Mark Greenberg/Visions, J.R. Eyerman/LIFE, Mark Kauffman **78** UPI/Corbis-Bettmann (2) **79** Fenno Jacobs/Black Star **80** UPI/Corbis-Bettmann (2) **81** Robert Phillips/LIFE **82** AP/Wide World, UPI/Corbis-Bettmann, Bohemia **83** Triangle Photo, John Sadovy/LIFE **84** Allan Grant/LIFE, Sovfoto **86** Don Wright, Hank Walker/LIFE **87** Dennis Stock/Magnum, Michael Ochs Archive, Hans Namuth **88** Tom Kelley/George Zeno Collection, Graphic House/Archive, UPI/Corbis-Bettmann **89** Jay:Leviton-Atlanta, Charles James Dawson/AP/Wide World, J.R. Eyerman/LIFE

REVOLUTION 90-91 Michael O'Sullivan **92-93** no credit, Marc Riboud/Magnum, Hap Stewart/Bethel, John S. Clarke/Camera Press/Retna **94** UPI/Corbis-Bettmann, Bill Eppridge/LIFE **95** Bob Adelman/Magnum, Charles Moore/Black Star **96** Larry Burrows **97** Art Shay, John A. Darnell/LIFE **98** John Dominis/LIFE, Li Zhensheng/M Photo, Peter Leibing/Conti-Press/AP/Wide World **100** Maj. James A. McDivitt/NASA **101** AP/Wide World (2) **102** ©Neil Leifer, Bill Eppridge/LIFE **103** Arthur Schatz **104** David Gahr, Peter L. Gould/Images **105** David Gahr, Ture Westberg-Tio, Arthur McEwen **106** Kurt Gunther/London Features, AP/Wide World (2) **107** Augusto Meneses, Mo Garcia, Henry Grossman

LIMITS 108 Bill Pierce **109** Hubert Van Es/UPI/Corbis-Bettmann **110-111** Steve Allen/The Image Bank, Ellis Herwig/Boston *Globe*, Bob Gruen, Christopher Springmann/Black Star, Ken Regan/Camera 5 **112** Mark Godfrey, David Hume Kennerly **113** Dennis Brack/Black Star, no credit **114** Alain Mingam/Gamma Liaison **115** D.B. Owen/Black Star, Phillip Jones Griffiths/Magnum **116** Steve Northup, Rog Wilson **117** Neil

Leifer **118** Annie Hagman, Eddie Adams **119** AP/Wide World **120** 20th Century Fox, ABC-TV, no credit, Ritch Barnes **121** Gorgoni/Contact Press, Martha Swope©Time Inc. **122** Svenskt Pressfoto, Lyn Goldsmith/Corbis, Martha Swope©Time Inc. **123** Mohamed Amin, John Barr/Gamma Liaison, Nancy Moran

COMEBACK 124 Anthony Suau/Gamma Liaison **125** Michael Evans/Gamma Liaison **126-127** Bill Fitzpatrick/The White House (Gorbachev and Reagan), Chip Hires/Gamma Liaison, no credit, George Lange/Outline Press **128** Terry Ashe/TIME, Dirck Halstead/TIME **129** DeWildenberg/Gamma Liaison, Peter Jordan **130** Alain Keler/Sygma, Kenneth Jarecke/Contact Press **131** James Nachtwey/Magnum **132** Bruce Weaver/AP/Wide World, Alon Reininger/Contact Press **133** Roger Werth/Woodfin Camp **134** Arthur Grace/Sygma, Raghu Rai/Magnum, Matthew Naythons **136** Neal Preston, Janette Beckman/Outline Press **137** John Napier, Aaron Rapoport/Outline Press, Hogan/Corbis **138** Douglas Kirkland/Sygma, David Burnett/Contact Press **139** Peter Jordan, Bob Galbraith/AP/Wide World, David Gamble

IMAGES 140 Diana Walker for TIME **141** J.L. Curtis, Diana Walker for TIME **142** Brooks Kraft/Sygma, P.F. Bentley for TIME (2) **143** Steve Liss for TIME, Rick Friedman, Steve Liss for TIME **144** James Nachtwey/Magnum for TIME, Eugene Pierce **145** James Nachtwey/Magnum for TIME (2) **146** Christopher Morris/Black Star for TIME, Mario Ruiz for TIME, Christopher Morris/Black Star for TIME **147** Mountain/The Guardian Angels, Anthony Suau for TIME

TRANSFORMATION 148-149 ©Louis Psihoyos/Matrix **150-151** Alexander Zemlianchenko/AP/Wide World, David Strick/Outline Press, Alan Schein/The Stock Market, Dennis Galante, Louise Gubb/The Image Works **152** Steve Liss for TIME, David Turnley/Black Star **153** Stephanie Compoint/Sygma **154** Greg Smith/Saba, Vince Bucci/Reuters/Archive **155** Charles H. Porter IV/Sygma **156** Barbara Kinney/The White House, Allan Tannenbaum/Sygma, Anthony Suau for TIME **158** Remi Benali & Stephen Ferry/Gamma Liaison, JPL/NASA **159** Hester & Paul Scowen/ASU/NASA **160** Jon Bernadez/Cover **161** Dana Lixenberg/Outline Press, Kurt Weddle/Sipa Press, Joan Marcus, Merie Wallace/Paramount Pictures/20th Century Fox **162** Pablo Bartholomew/Gamma Liaison, Todd Korol/Sipa Press, Joe McNally/LIFE **163** Noren Trotman/NBA Photos, Jack Smith/AP/Wide World, David Burnett/Contact

ESSAY 164-165 (illustration) Chip Kidd for TIME

BACK COVER (right to left, from top) Hulton Getty/Tony Stone Images, Brown Brothers, U.S. Army/AP/Wide World, Don Wright, Michael O'Sullivan, Bill Pierce, Anthony Suau/Gamma Liaison, © Louise Gubb/The Image Works